CRUEL
AND
UNUSUAL
JUSTICE

OTHER BOOKS BY JACK NEWFIELD

A Prophetic Minority (1966)
Robert Kennedy: A Memoir (1969)
Bread and Roses Too (1971)
A Populist Manifesto (1972) with Jeff Greenfield

CRUEL AND UNUSUAL JUSTICE

JACK NEWFIELD

HOLT, RINEHART AND WINSTON
NEW YORK / CHICAGO / SAN FRANCISCO

Copyright © 1974 by Jack Newfield
All rights reserved, including the right to reproduce
this book or portions thereof in any form.
Published simultaneously in Canada by Holt, Rinehart
and Winston of Canada, Limited.

Library of Congress Cataloging in Publication Data
Newfield, Jack.
    Cruel and unusual justice.
    1. Criminal justice, Administration of—New York (State)
    I. Title.
KFN6102.N49   345′.747′05   73–4202
ISBN 0–03–011041–6

First Edition
Designer: Vincent Torre
Printed in the United States of America

Grateful acknowledgment is made to *The Village Voice* for permission to reprint the following in somewhat revised form: "The Law Is an Outlaw" (December 17, 1970); "A Tale of Two Jails" (January 21, 1971); "It's All Death Row" (September 2, 1971); "Parody of Progress" (December 2, 1971); "Ghetto of Pain" (December 30, 1971); "Clinton Prison" (February 17, 1972); "Justice Gets a Fix" (August 31, 1972); "Judge Corso and the Mafia" (October 12, 1972); "The Politics of Justice" (November 9, 1972); "Seven Suspicious Cases" (November 30, 1972); "The Life and Hard Times of Judge Aaron Koota" (December 28, 1972); "'Mindlessly, randomly, hurriedly, blindly'" (February 8, 1973); "A Decent Judge in a Rotten System" (March 1, 1973); "Scavengers of the System" (March 29, 1973). Reprinted by permission of The Village Voice. Copyrighted by The Village Voice, Inc., 1970, 1971, 1972, 1973.

"Anniversary for Attica" first appeared under the title of "An Anniversary for Attica" in *The New York Times* of September 13, 1972. © 1972 by The New York Times Company. Reprinted by permission.

"'Remember Attica,'" © 1971 by Jack Newfield, first appeared under the title of "City Politic: Remember Attica" in *New York* Magazine of September 27, 1971, issue 39, volume 4.

"'I am Attica,'" © 1972 by Jack Newfield, first appeared under the title of "'I Am Attica'—The Trials of Herbert X. Blyden" in *New York* Magazine of May 15, 1972, issue 20, volume 5.

"The Ten Worst Judges in New York," © 1972 by Jack Newfield, first appeared in *New York* Magazine of October 16, 1972, issue 42, volume 5.

First the sentence, then the trial.

—Alice in Wonderland

In the halls of justice, the only justice is in the halls.

—Lenny Bruce

See how yond justice rails upon yond simple thief. Hark in thine ear. Change places: and, handy-dandy, which is the justice, which is the thief?

—Shakespeare, *King Lear*

Contents

Acknowledgments

There are some people I would like to thank for their generous and valuable enlightenment while I was working on this book.

Tom Santise, Jerry McKenna, Bill vanden Heuvel, David Durk, Adam Walinsky, Terry Lenzner, Martin Garbus, Irving Younger, Dave Rothenberg, Len Sandler, Bobby Brownstein, Jack Weinstein, Jim Leff, Nick Scopetta, Mario Cuomo, Larry Cole, Joe Hynes, Bob Morgenthau, Henry Ruth, and Bill Goodstein.

If everyone in the criminal justice system were like them, there would be no need to write a book like this.

Introduction

THE CRIMINAL JUSTICE MAZE in New York City does not work; to call its disintegrating parts a "system" would be flattery. This book tries to describe the maze and show its contribution to both the fact of crime and the fear of crime.

Street crime obviously has many causes: Poverty, heroin addiction, organized crime (the ITT of heroin distribution), human nature, corruption within law enforcement are all factors. And so is the fact that our prisons and courts—as institutions—are failures.

Prisons don't rehabilitate. Prisons don't deter; 70 percent of all crimes are committed by ex-offenders. Prisons dehumanize. They punish. They embitter. They damage. Prisons are conceived as garbage dumps. So long as they are far away, few of us want to know what really goes on behind the tall, gray walls. And because there is no outside scrutiny, those who run the prisons feel free to do what they want.

Prisons like Attica and Clinton are built in remote places, far from cities; they are staffed by people from the local area —mostly rural, mostly white. When the riot began at Attica, there was not one black correction officer on the staff of the prison. Every correction officer was white and rural. Yet most of the inmates were nonwhite and urban. With such a chasm of communication, even if there had been a concept of rehabilitation it would have been doomed.

The courts, too, do not work. They do not provide prompt trials or equal justice, as guaranteed by the Constitution.

Blacks receive longer sentences than whites, and defendants with private lawyers are twice as likely not to go to jail as defendants with court-appointed lawyers.

Most penologists and criminologists now believe that it is the *certainty* of sentence, not the *severity* of sentence, that is the real deterrent to crime. But two recent studies by the Joint Legislative Committee on Crime suggest that heroin dealers and Mafia members face no certainty of punishment in New York's courts.

The Joint Committee examined the dispositions of 1,762 Mafia defendants between 1960 and 1970. Of these Mafiosi, 44.7 percent received dismissals or acquittals. Only 11.5 percent of the indictments against all other defendants were dismissed.

The committee also studied the 2,500 sentences given major narcotics violators between October of 1969 and September of 1971. Only 34 percent of those junk dealers convicted of a felony—possession of more than a pound of heroin or cocaine—received prison terms of more than one year; 26 percent were sentenced to less than a year. And a staggering 40 percent were discharged, paroled, fined, or placed on probation—in short, returned to the community after being convicted of a crime for which they could have gotten a life sentence under the existing State Penal Law.

The committee's work disclosed that in the last two years, thirty convicted heroin dealers in New York City received illegal sentences from judges—conditional or unconditional discharges for felony narcotics crimes. Section 65.05 of the State Penal Law specifically prohibits a judge from giving such a sentence.

Justice is also distorted by considerations of economic class.

On September 18, 1973, Jack Clark, the corporate chairman of the Four Seasons Nursing Centers of America, was sentenced for stock fraud. Clark had cheated shareholders out of $200 million, and according to U.S. Attorney Paul Curran, Clark had personally "profited by $10 million," and he had "stashed" another $4 million in a secret Delaware trust.

Clark could have received five years in prison. U.S. Attorney Curran asked for "appropriate punishment because it is vitally important that the rich and powerful not be given preferential treatment which is not accorded to the blue-collar worker."

Nevertheless, Clark was sentenced to one year in prison, which meant he became eligible for parole after four months.

The next day, in Brooklyn Supreme Court, an eighteen-year-old Puerto Rican named Hector Ortiz was sentenced to five years in prison for stealing a car worth $100—and he was not accused of using violence or a gun.

In the federal courts in 1971, 71 percent of all defendants convicted of auto theft went to prison, for an average sentence of three years. In contrast, only 16 percent of those defendants convicted of securities fraud went to prison, for an average term of nineteen months.

In New York's courts, law and justice have become subordinated to politics and patronage. State Supreme Court justices are picked in private negotiations between the county leaders of both political parties. Past favors, the opening up of a City Council seat or an Assembly seat, and cash contributions to the party treasury seem to be the standards for making a judge. Knowledge of the law, honesty, commitment to the Constitution seem to be far from County Leader Meade Esposito's mind when he makes a judge. Of the last hundred Supreme Court justices "elected" in New York City, ninety-one had both Democratic and Republican endorsement. Some judges even had the endorsement of all four political parties, yet were found unqualified by the Bar Association.

The context for the articles in this book is a climate of corruption prevailing throughout the criminal justice maze in New York City. (Watergate, the milk-fund, Agnew, ITT, and other scandals have, of course, been part of the larger national context of corruption.)

On December 28, 1972, the 264-page Knapp Commission report on police corruption was released. The report, the result of eighteen months of investigative work and two sets of public hearings, concluded that a "sizeable majority" of the city's 30,000 policemen participated in some form of graft. But, though this generalization got the headlines, the specifics of the heroin corruption, as detailed in the report, were more sickening.

Police conduct that the Knapp Commission report described as "typical" and "numerous" included:

—cops selling heroin;

—cops selling information to dealers and accepting heroin in payment;

—cops protecting heroin dealers by registering them as informants;

—cops financing heroin transactions;

—cops selling the identity of police informants to the Mafia;

—cops kidnapping important witnesses to prevent them from testifying at the trials of major heroin dealers;

—cops providing protection ("riding shotgun") for heroin dealers;

—cops providing "hit men" to kill potential witnesses.

The Knapp report went on to describe how the highest officials in a "reform" city administration refused to act on information about this corruption offered by two honest cops, Frank Serpico and David Durk, more than three years before the formation of the Knapp Commission.

Arnold Fraiman was then the city's investigations commissioner, the official directly responsible for looking into any allegation of misconduct. The Knapp report said of him, "Fraiman failed to take the action that was clearly called for in a situation which seemed to involve the most serious kinds of corruption ever to come to the attention of his office, and which seemed to be precisely the sort of case his office was set up to handle."

Arnold Fraiman is now a judge.

Five weeks after the release of the Knapp report, before most of us could fully digest its narrative details, the news broke that $73 million worth of heroin and cocaine (398 pounds) had been stolen from the Police Department's storage rooms.

There is other evidence to indicate the dimensions of the corruption of the law in New York City.

Thomas Mackell has been indicted for obstruction of justice and forced to resign as district attorney of Queens.

In the past two years, one Supreme Court justice—Seymour Thaler—has been convicted of a felony, and another —Mitchell Schweitzer—has been forced to retire under threat of a judicial trial.

In the past fifteen months, more than a hundred policemen have been arrested on charges of corruption, and thirty-nine more have been suspended from the force.

The 1972 annual report of the State Commission of Investigation found that "corruption is significant throughout the entire system of criminal justice, especially in the area of narcotics."

The Knapp Commission, as valuable as it has been, was limited by its mandate. Unfortunately, the commission only probed the working-class segment of the criminal justice maze—the police. It left the judges, the district attorneys, and the lawyers alone. One of the basic objectives of this book is to raise the level of scrutiny to the respectable elite —to the judges and to those "superjudges" who administer the courts.

A cop, a black cop in the ghetto, told me how he locked up a heroin dealer one night. The dealer had $16,000 in cash on him. The cop had $14 in his wallet and earned $11,000 a year. The dealer offered the cop all $16,000 to cut him loose. The cop said no. And the junk dealer said, "Don't be a fool. If you don't take it, the judge will."

Until a commission, equivalent in authority to the Knapp Commission, is set up to investigate the judiciary as fully, little will change.

Introduction

A final word.

This is a journalist's book. It is a book made out of experience, research, facts, and outrage. There is little theory or philosophy in it.

But there are certain basic values that form the foundation for the journalism. These values come from many sources—from Jefferson, from Brandeis, from Martin Luther King, from Edmond Cahn, and most importantly, from the Constitution and the Bill of Rights. They are values of democracy, due process, equal protection under the rule of law, and social justice.

These root values seem to me more significant than the specific proposals for court and prison reform that are scattered throughout these pages. It is easy to assert a program. It is all there in political speeches and foundation studies and commission reports with names like Knapp, McKay, and Kerner.

But it is the underlying egalitarian and humanist values that are so totally absent from the prisons and courtrooms I visited over the last three years.

The carnage at Attica, the bedlam of the Tombs, the lower courts that resemble broken meat grinders—these are symptoms of a system bereft of moral or constitutional sense.

The absence of equal justice and due process, the presence of corruption and cruelty—these exist because there is no passion for justice.

JACK NEWFIELD
Autumn, 1973

PRISONS

"The only way we're ever going to get prison reform is when we get a higher class of prisoner."

—Tombs inmate

The Law Is
an Outlaw

"We have no mouth and we
must scream."
—An anonymous inmate
shouting out of a
broken window
in the Tombs.

IT WAS ABOUT 7:45 A.M. on Monday, October 5, 1970.
New York's Mayor Lindsay and his press secretary Tom
Morgan were inside meeting with the inmates of the Long
Island City Men's House of Detention after they had ended
their revolt peacefully. Released hostages were telling reporters on the sidewalk outside that the inmates had pro-
tected them, had saved their lives, and that the basic
demands of the rebels—lower bail, speedier trials, less
overcrowding—were just.

It was 7:45 A.M. when correction officers—mostly white
—began to beat prisoners—mostly black—who had been
promised no reprisals by the warden. The correction officers
began to systematically club the prisoners in the courtyard
of the eighty-six-year-old brick jail with ax handles, baseball
bats, and riot sticks. They beat them so savagely that a

photographer from the New York *Daily News* vomited at the sight of the flowing blood and cracking bones.

Michael McCardell is a reporter for the *Daily News*. He witnessed the beatings from the ninth-floor window of a factory-warehouse that looked down on the courtyard. In the next morning's *Daily News,* this is how he described what he saw:

It was a gruesome scene.

About 250 prisoners were sitting on the grass. Behind them, 30 Correction Department guards were lined up, all of them holding weapons—ax handles, baseball bats, and night sticks.

One inmate was dragged out a doorway onto a loading platform and five guards attacked him with their clubs. They battered his head and blood flowed over his face and body. He was kicked off the platform and several other guards pounded him again with their clubs.

His limp form then was lifted off the ground and thrown into a bus as another prisoner was hauled out and belted across the back with a club. Then more clubs rained down on him until he was motionless and blood-soaked. He too was thrown into the bus.

Another man was pushed out, his hands above his head. A bat caught him in the stomach and he doubled over. More clubs came down on his spine. Eight guards were slugging away at one time.

A fourth prisoner emerged but the guards seemed to let go of him. He began running but the guards caught him and one put a knee into his groin. He toppled over and more guards kicked him over and over.

Six more prisoners got the same treatment.

A police official who would not give his name was asked about the beatings. "We don't know," he replied. "That's Correction Department domain. We're only here if they need us."

It was 7:45 A.M. then and Lindsay had been in the prison

since 6:20. From behind police barricades one could see the prisoner-occupied east wing of the sixth floor.

Victor Martinez, a leader of the insurrection, leaned out and shouted through a megaphone: "Prisoners are being beaten. They are being killed. The mayor is lying."

Lindsay left at 8.20 A.M. Asked about the beatings, he said, "I have been told there were injuries on both sides."

When Tom Morgan left the jail that morning after seventy-two sleepless hours, reporters told him about the beatings. He just couldn't believe it. Later he saw the dark, grainy films on television and was sickened by them. Another Lindsay aide, Barry Gottehrer, who had helped negotiate the settlement with the inmates, was so heartbroken by the brutality that he had to leave town on a vacation to get his emotions back in order. After Mayor Lindsay learned about the beatings, he directed Correction Commissioner George McGrath to submit a "full and speedy" report on the incident. He also asked Corporation Counsel J. Lee Rankin to look into the matter.

Three weeks after the beatings, Queens District Attorney Thomas Mackell anticipated the inverted justice at Kent State by announcing the indictment of eight inmates, seven of them black, two of them Panthers. He exonerated all the guards, despite the substantial film and photographic evidence. The inmates were indicted on such charges as kidnapping, attempted larceny, and conspiracy.

That was in October. Time passes and people forget. New outrages now compete for our attention. Meanwhile, all journalists have been barred by Commissioner McGrath from monitoring the city's jails. The appropriate speeches and editorials urging six-point or ten-point court and penal reforms have been churned out, duly noted, and filed away. Once again there is no communication between the outside world and the municipal Cancer Wards. The inmates continued to suffer worse food, worse health care, and less space than the animals caged in the Central Park Zoo. But until the next riot, it is no longer news.

Two months after the beatings, I telephoned the office of Commissioner McGrath to see if he had yet submitted his "full and speedy" report to the mayor.

"What report?" asked the commissioner's press secretary, Al Castro.

"The one about correction officers beating up inmates with ax handles two months ago," I answered.

"What are you, some wise guy? No one got hit with any ax handles. I don't know when that report will be finished."

I repeated this conversation to William vanden Heuvel, who had only recently been appointed chairman of the New York City Board of Correction, a citizens' watchdog agency, and asked him to ascertain the status of McGrath's report.

The next day vanden Heuvel told me he had been informed by McGrath that the "full and speedy" report was not yet even half finished, and might not be completed for two more months.

Kew Gardens is another jail in Queens. There too, in October, 1970, prisoners rioted, surrendered on the promise of no reprisals, and were beaten. But these beatings were administered in secret behind the stone walls, days after the trouble was over. The brutality was so total, so systematic, it can be described fairly as torture.

Four young lawyers for the Legal Aid Society—William

Hellerstein, Barbara Shapiro, William Nelson, and Joel Berger—have now collected sworn affidavits from the victims. (Several of these inmates were indicted by Queens District Attorney Mackell on sodomy, bribery, and other felony charges right after they began to talk to Legal Aid Society lawyers about their plight.) These statements read as if they had been smuggled out of Brazil, or Greece, or Stalin's labor camps. But they came from New York City and have now been submitted to the Eastern District Court in a class-action lawsuit on behalf of the 800 inmates against Mayor Lindsay, Commissioner McGrath, Kew Gardens Warden John Kennedy, and Deputy Warden Albert Ossakow.

The suit was argued before Justice Orin Judd. The lawyer who represented the Correction Department, Irwin Herzog, is the same lawyer who was authorized to investigate the Correction Department's conduct at the Long Island City jail for the corporation counsel, J. Lee Rankin.

Somehow neither the affidavits nor the case has been noticed by the daily press. But they are important if unpleasant reading, and several of these simple, dignified accounts, all from citizens who assert they did not participate in the revolt and did not resist when it was over, are quoted here at some length.

From Jonathan Williams:

"The officers were shooting more gas onto the floor at this time [October 3]. Inmates were hollering, 'We give up.' I heard people screaming things like this: 'Don't hit me no more,' 'We give up,' 'Oh my God, my head.'

"Then the COs [correction officers] came onto Upper D where I was lying in a corner. . . .

"As I went downstairs, as ordered, the officers were hitting me and all the other prisoners with nightsticks and ax handles. As I came off the steps an officer drew his club back to hit me on the head. I put my arm up to protect my head and the blow hit my right arm, breaking it. . . .

"I saw people bleeding profusely from the head. I saw one man with a bloody towel around his head trying to get up to get a fresh towel. . . . The COs then ordered us to chant, 'Power to the COs.' If you didn't say it, you would get beaten. One Spanish boy from the Upper D gallery who couldn't understand a word of English got beaten because he did not say, 'Power to the COs.'

"Around 8 or 9 A.M. Sunday morning [October 4], we were put into cells, three or four to a cell. . . . Happy Gray was put on Upper C side, where a man died of head wounds. [Correction officers claimed the inmate died of an 'overdose of Darvon.']

"After a cast was put on my arm I was in the custody of a CO named P. Baily, handcuffed to him. This was early Tuesday morning, October 6, and I had had nothing to eat since the sandwich early Sunday morning. . . .

"We were taken from the bullpen to the third floor 'bing' [solitary] on Tuesday afternoon. . . . I was in the cell for about an hour when the beatings began again. I heard about a dozen beatings. One man was hit with a stick across the knees and fell down opposite my cell. The COs beat him until his head opened up.

"This continued through Tuesday night. On Thursday or Friday [October 8 or 9] I saw many inmates, naked, being beaten in the dayroom. . . . I have been kept in the bing all this time. I am locked in my cell 24 hours a day. I have gotten no mail from my wife, and I am unable to write to my two children. I know that my wife has written to me. . . . In over three weeks I have been allowed only one shower. All my clothes and other possessions were taken from me, including my mail and my pictures of my family.

"About 18 days after I was put in the bing, deputy warden Schaeffer came around and gave everyone an envelope and one sheet of paper. He said we could write to our families and tell them everything was all right with us. I wrote my wife telling her my arm was broken and asking her to send a lawyer to see me. No lawyer has come, and I am sure the letter was not mailed."

Donald Leroland's affidavit:

"Late Saturday night or early Sunday morning Warden Kennedy spoke over the public address system, telling everyone to lock in their cells and turn their lights on as a signal of surrender. He said that if this were done there would be no reprisals. I locked in and turned my light on. . . .

"During the next few days many men were brought down from the floors above, beaten with sticks and clubs. . . .

"Friday, October 9, 20 or 30 COs came onto my gallery and ordered everyone to strip naked. We were then marched, hands over heads, into the dayroom. . . . In the dayroom I was lined up with about 40–45 other inmates in three rows, facing a wall. Deputy Warden Ossakow ordered us to turn around and face him, saying, 'I want to see if any of my friends are here.'

"Officer McCoy then said, 'Everybody line up, pricks to asses. Everyone who gets a hard-on can walk' [meaning anyone who got an erection would not be beaten].

"McCoy then started beating everyone in the back row with a club on their buttocks and legs. . . . The physical beating was not as painful as the humiliation."

Ralph Valvano's affidavit:

"From what I heard there was no resistance by the prisoners on the fourth floor, that no resistance was possible. The guards came in and brutally beat the prisoners. I heard the screaming and the next day the injured were taken to the third floor. In all about 40 prisoners were beaten. . . . A man named Rabbi is still in Kings County Hospital with a broken leg. Someone named Shorty, a black man, was killed. Although the guards said he died of an overdose, he was seen in a sheet with his head wide open, and the sheet with large red stains by at least two men: Raymond Minori and Happy Gray. . . .

"From Sunday, October 4, to Friday, October 9, the entire prison population was subjected to beatings. I heard many screams and saw with my own eyes three men, naked, being beaten with sticks down the stairs, in three separate incidents. . . . The official in charge of these beatings was Captain Hall.

"On Monday, October 5, I was put in the bing, or segregation. No reason was given. I was locked in 24 hours a day, with no mattress, no visiting rights, and I can neither send nor receive mail. For the first 10 days I was without blankets. My cell is 3 LC 9. . . .

"On October 18, one of the prisoners, Richard Tucker, swallowed glass in order to get out of the prison. He was badly beaten, taken to Kings County Hospital, and beaten again when he returned.

"I have been threatened with an indictment for leading

the riot by Captain Hall. Deputy Warden Ossakow told me, 'Valvano, I'm going to get you without even laying a hand on you.' "

Richard Flower's affidavit:

"I don't know what happened to Sonny Sheara. Another correction officer came by shortly after this beating and said to me, 'It's a damn shame the warden ordered these beatings.' This particular correction officer did not take part in the beating and he was put on 12-hour turnkey duty as punishment. . . .

"The evening of October 5, Monday, we were herded into the dayroom, naked. A correction officer ordered us to stand closer: 'I want your dick in the man's ass in front of you,' he said. 'Anyone whose dick gets hard, you walk without a beating.' I can identify the correction officer who made this order, but I do not know his name. Captain Hal' was present."

There are a dozen more statements like these, describing wounds not treated, warnings not to talk to Legal Aid Society lawyers, the confiscation of inmates' letters, pictures, and lawbooks, reprisals against guards horrified by the cruelty, days in the bing without toilet paper or blankets or solid food, and sadistic beatings committed in front of Deputy Warden Ossakow.

On November 12, Ralph Valvano dictated a supplemental statement to a Legal Aid lawyer. It concluded: "I am frightened of losing my life. I find the constant intimidation and abuse almost unbearable. I wish to state here that I have no intention of harming myself—if I come to harm it will be because the guards have harmed me."

A few facts to meditate on. Almost all the inmates of the

Kew Gardens jail, of the Tombs, and of the Long Island City Men's House of Detention have not been convicted of a crime. According to the Constitution, they are innocent until proven guilty by a jury. These institutions are detention facilities, not punishment prisons. The men are detained there usually because they could not raise the $500 or $1,000 bail on the single phone call they are allowed. Most of them have been in these dungeons for six and twelve months waiting for their trials to begin, 25 percent on bail of $500 or less. Under any name, this is preventive detention. They rot in these Cancer Wards because they are poor and because some judges are political hacks who work only three hours a day. Most of these same judges are opposed to the penal reform supported by Chief Justice Burger and Mayor Lindsay and already adopted by the state of California, the reform that places a sixty-day legal limit on the time between arrest and trial.

Even before the first prison riots in August, 1970, the conditions in these detention facilities were subhuman. The Tombs that summer was 900 prisoners above its 930 capacity. The Kew Gardens detention center, with a capacity of 520, held more than 1,000 inmates. During the riots, the bodies of giant dead rats were hurled through the broken shards of glass in the Tombs down onto the sidewalk. The city's entire correction system has only two exterminators on its payroll. And there are eleven part-time psychiatrists for the approximately 10,000 prisoners.

Today, after all the promises and publicity, nothing has changed. Vague speeches about future court, bail, and penal reforms do not affect daily life in the dungeons. The bing cells, as infamous as the tiger cages of South Vietnam, are still used in all the city's detention facilities without comment by the press. Inmate suicides continue to take place, with increasingly less space given over to them in the newspapers. Commissioner McGrath has rejected modest requests by Father Laurence Gibney (the chaplain at the Tombs) that the inmates be given more than one uniform for their entire stay in jail, that there be more law books in the prison library so they might help prepare their own defense, that reporters be given permission to visit and monitor the jails, and that inmates be permitted more than one phone call to raise bail. (In 1968, the Vera Institute of Justice and the Mayor's Criminal Justice Coordinating Council conducted a study that showed that a prisoner with direct access to a telephone was twice as likely to make bail and suggested that such access would ease the crisis of overcrowding.)

"We have no mouth and we must scream," the anonymous voice screamed from the Tombs. But there is no one now behind the walls to hear the mouthless voices.

It is always difficult to isolate accountability in a case like this, where there is a closed cycle of error. Who is to blame? Is it the individual guards? The warden? Commissioner McGrath? District Attorney Mackell? The nameless, impersonal thing called "the system"?

Why did Commissioner McGrath cover up these beatings? Why hasn't Lindsay fired McGrath, whose four-year tenure in office has been characterized by riots, brutality, and suicides? How could Corporation Counsel Rankin permit the lawyer investigating the Correction Department behavior at the Long Island City jail to represent the Correction Department in the court hearing on the Kew Gardens jail?

Perhaps the answer is that legal authority in New York has become as corrupt as in the film *Z*. Once, a long time ago in Mississippi, SNCC organizer Bob Moses asked me, after Goodman, Chaney, and Schwerner had been murdered by the local sheriff, "What do you do when the law is an outlaw?"

More and more that question haunts me. It was the National Guard who killed the four students at Kent State. It was the Chicago police who murdered Fred Hampton. Here in two New York jails, it was the guards and the wardens who broke the law, and so far no one seems interested in remedying this parody of law and order.

The law is an outlaw. And all the mouthless voices are screaming behind the thick walls for justice.

December 17, 1970

POSTSCRIPT

When I first published the affidavits from the inmates of the Kew Gardens jail, Correction Commissioner McGrath said on a television program that I was "irresponsible" and the sworn statements were "all lies."

In July of 1971, United States Magistrate Vincent Catoggio dismissed a class-action lawsuit based on these affidavits, concluding that the inmates' charges of brutality were "a gigantic hoax and fraud."

But Federal Judge Orin Judd then appointed thirty-four-year-old lawyer Stanley Arkin to conduct his own inquiry into the events in the Kew Gardens jail.

On January 2, 1973, Arkin's fifty-page report was released. The Arkin report accused Warden Ossakow and ten correction officers of using unnecessary and excessive physical force on inmates. Warden Ossakow was cited for the specific violation of fifty-four departmental regulations.

The end result, however, was less than satisfactory. Warden Ossakow was permitted to plead guilty at a departmental trial and to retire quietly. He was fined $600—one week's pay. And he was allowed to keep his pension of $20,000 a year.

A more appropriate punishment might have been a month's sentence in the Kew Gardens jail.

A Tale of
Two Jails

"I suspect that all the crimes
committed by all the jailed
criminals do not equal in social damage that of the crimes
committed against them."
—Dr. Karl Menninger,
The Crime of Punishment

A TALE of two jails, one federal, the other municipal,
one the responsibility of the U.S. Attorney General, the
other the responsibility of Mayor John Lindsay.

On January 5, 1971, two days after a small riot, Congressman Edward Koch and I spent three hours inspecting
the Federal House of Detention at 427 West Street near
11th Street in Manhattan. It is old, overcrowded, and under-
staffed. But it is, on balance, one of the less dehumanizing
jails in the country. Inmates voluntarily told us that the
new warden, Louis Gengler, was "humane," "honest," "liberal." One even said he'd sent the warden a Christmas card.

Warden Gengler permitted Koch and me to go into the
cells alone to talk to inmates; no guards were present. One
inmate told me, "I've been in the Tombs, in Brooklyn, in
Newark, and this is paradise."

Inmates told us there was no brutality, they got clean underwear three times a week, the food was "okay," and they had a gym to work out in. One of them said: "The warden comes around twice a day and asks us for our complaints. He tries to do what he can for us." Other inmates told us that there were law books in the library and that common-law wives and friends were allowed to visit them on holidays. The inmates were permitted to leave their cells and walk around the cell block during the day.

At one point Koch asked a famous alleged Mafioso if he had any grievances about the jail, and the man answered, "Just that we don't have girls and weekend passes. . . . This is a very decent joint." When I asked another group of about twelve inmates who were playing cards in one cell if they had any complaints, the only one offered was the absence of kosher food. Again, this conversation was conducted with no guards within hearing distance.

The visit persuaded me that despite antiquated physical facilities and insufficient funds, despite slow courts and unfair bail, a relatively humane administration is still possible within the rotting shell of the existing criminal justice system.

When Koch returned to his office he drafted a letter to Norman Carlson, director of the Bureau of Prisons. In it Koch wrote: "Over the past two years I have visited four prisons in New York City and elsewhere, and I must tell you that no other wardens in any other prison that I visited had the same laudatory comments made about them as did Warden Gengler. . . . In my opinion he is doing an excellent job in spite of the handicaps."

It was not easy getting a view inside a New York City jail. My first request to visit a detention facility, made in December, 1970, was rejected by Commissioner McGrath. A tour, with Congressman Koch, scheduled for January 13, 1971, was canceled at the last minute. John Parsons of CBS-TV was promised an "open door" tour of the Tombs the same week, but was not permitted to talk to inmates or to see the isolation cell. A tour of Kew Gardens for about forty-five print and television reporters that week also excluded any direct contact with inmates. I insisted that any legitimate tour must include access to inmates, as had my visit to the Federal House of Detention.

Finally, on Monday of the following week, Representative Koch, Representative Joseph Adabbo of Queens, and I were given a two-hour tour of the Kew Gardens jail by Commissioner McGrath. This, the newest of the city's six detention jails, was completed in 1962. On the outside it looks impressive with its clean new bricks and modern design.

Inside, the human part of it, is another story. The prison holds 530 inmates. About half of the jail population is awaiting trial; most have been waiting for more than four months. They are locked in their cells twenty-one hours a day. For three hours they are permitted to congregate in the narrow corridors outside their cells. They have no recreation facilities whatever, no radios, not even checker games. They have no methadone withdrawal treatment for narcotics addicts, and about 60 percent of all the inmates are addicts. One part-time psychiatrist, on duty nine hours a week, services all the 530 inmates.

We first visited a tier of cells on the fifth floor. About fifteen inmates were sitting in the four-foot-wide corridor, as part of their "recreation time" outside their six-by-eight cells. Congressman Koch asked them if they had any complaints.

One man, about forty-five years old, said in broken English that he had been wearing the same underwear and the same pants ever since he was arrested six months ago. He said he had no family to bring him clean clothes. "I've asked the guards to get me clean underwear," he said, "but they don't listen."

Warden Ossakow, who looks and sounds like the comedian Phil Foster, said, "Maybe his English isn't understandable." When I asked how many of the guards speak Spanish, he said, "Two, and one is the cashier in the commissary."

We next spoke to a narcotics addict in his cell. "I came in here sick as a dog," he began. "I'm a junkie. I stayed awake for twenty-five days. I didn't eat for fourteen days. I asked the guard to let me see a doctor, but they wouldn't let me. I belong in a hospital. I need methadone. I kicked heroin here alone. I was in agony. The guard told me there was no doctor available. They only gave me tranquilizers."

Koch, who was instrumental in obtaining a twenty-bed methadone withdrawal program at the Tombs jail, repeated the man's story to Commissioner McGrath, who said, "I can't believe it."

At the end of the tour we went down to the medical office to look up the inmate's record. It consisted of a blue card with information filled in.

"You see, he's lying," McGrath said.

Koch, examining the record closely, said, "He's not lying,

Commissioner. Look here." Koch then showed the commissioner that the story the inmate had told us of being arrested in Brooklyn and then being transferred to Queens was substantiated. The blue card described the prisoner as a "four bundles a day" heroin addict, but "not in withdrawal." It showed no record of medical treatment, except for tranquilizers, since his admission to the jail. (There was one part of the card that neither Koch nor McGrath could decipher.)

"This man belongs in a hospital!" Koch exclaimed.

The commissioner and the warden could offer no response.

The next inmate we talked to was also an addict. He said he had been in his cell for the last four days and had no soap, no razor, and no towel.

"All he has to do is just ask for a towel," said Ossakow. Koch asked the guard (black) if the prisoner had in fact requested a towel.

"Yes, he did," said the guard, "and I told the A Officer about it." However, the A Officer (white) claimed he had received no such request for a towel. The inmate said, "If I can't get a towel with the commissioner standing right here, what chance do I have when he's not around?"

Later, when Koch suggested to the warden that the second guard was lying, Ossakow replied, "Let's just say he was fearful of making a mistake."

Similar absurdities were apparent at other points of the visit. One inmate complained that he had not been permitted to receive visits from his common-law wife. The warden said the inmate had to "fill out a slip" for that privilege.

Then the inmate explained that he was told there were no more of those particular slips available to be filled out.

When Koch asked why prisoners in the bing were not allowed mattresses, he was told that was to prevent suicides. When Koch asked why drug addicts were not placed in a dormitory rather than the six-by-eight cells, he was told that "suicides were more likely in dormitories." ("Nonsense," Koch said later.)

At the end of the tour I remarked to mayoral aide Michael Dontzin that it all seemed crazy to me, particularly that the most modern of all the city's jails was without dormitories or hospital facilities. Dontzin said: "Of course this is all crazy. Kew Gardens is a maximum-security prison, and half the people in it have never been convicted. An idiot designed this jail. In 1962 Wagner was the mayor."

When the tour was completed I asked Koch to compare the physically deteriorated federal jail with the brand new city jail.

"Of course the federal jail is much better," Koch replied. "It's totally different there because the warden is a good human being. There is a different attitude here in Kew Gardens. Basic indignities are committed against inmates here. There is a bad attitude here, and it is compounded because they want to hide things here. But Kew Gardens represents the normal corrections mentality. Gengler is the exception."

There's almost nothing new I can say about this city's jails. (Kew Gardens, remember, is the best.) Everyone who cares now knows these are zoos where 6,000 men and women waiting for trials are rotting because they are too poor to make bail, and where they are subject to the most brutalizing conditions imaginable. Cold turkey, dirty clothes, no towels, no recreation, locked in their cells twenty-one hours a day. Ten years ago, editorials in *The New York Times* called the city's detention jails "dehumanizing" and "barbaric." But nothing has changed. It is as if the riots never happened.

There comes a time when even a writer—perhaps especially a writer—feels that words are worthless. The situation with the jails is now comparable to Germany in 1943 in the sense that there can be no more good New Yorkers; no one can pretend any longer that he is ignorant of what is happening behind the walls.

We all know it is a horror and a scandal. We know men have been stripped naked and beaten; we have seen the photographs of inmates having limbs smashed by baseball bats and ax handles. We know there have been seventeen suicides during the last twenty-four months. We know inmates have been beaten and prosecuted after all the official promises of no reprisals.

We don't need any more studies or articles or committees. We know all there is to know. No more words of shame, no more words of regret, no more words of anger. Only action.

January 21, 1971

It's All Death Row

NOBODY even remembers their names.

George James was twenty-one years old. He hung himself in the Tombs on January 7, 1971, with strips from a torn bedsheet. He was a heavy heroin addict and belonged in a hospital.

Robert Cruz was also twenty-one years old. He committed suicide in February at Rikers Island by hanging himself with his own shirt. Eight hours before he hung himself, Cruz had tried to slash his wrists, but the prison staff had decided he "was not suicidal." When *The New York Times* asked Al Castro, the press spokesman for the Correction Department, why the media were not informed of Cruz's death, Castro replied, "It was just a regular suicide, nothing special."

Harvey Smith killed himself at Rikers Island four days after Cruz. Smith was an epileptic and a heroin addict and had spent nine years in a mental hospital in Ohio. But the prison doctor refused to send him to Bellevue Hospital. He was alone in his cell at 5:30 A.M. when he hung himself with a noose fashioned out of bedsheets.

Alan Butler died in March at the Tombs. He died of pneumonia because the prison doctor did not give him his medicine. He was scheduled to be released the day he died.

William Waren was only eighteen years old. He was in Rikers Island because he couldn't raise $1,000 bail. He hung himself with a towel on August 15, 1971. He had tried to kill himself before but was not placed in a hospital.

Bernard Cintron died on August 10 at the Brooklyn House of Detention. The night Cintron died, Correction Commissioner George McGrath personally called *The New York Times* to explain that Cintron had attacked two guards with a knife and was fatally injured when the guards disarmed him. And that's how the *Times* wrote the story. McGrath told the same story to William vanden Heuvel, chairman of the citizens' watchdog agency over the prisons.

The truth about Cintron's death came out when Brooklyn District Attorney Eugene Gold disclosed that Cintron died as a result of a "homicidal assault" by four correction officers. Gold said that Cintron did not have a knife and that he did not attack the guards.

According to Gold: "The autopsy revealed that Cintron suffered multiple bruises of the face, forehead, scalp, left shoulder, left arm, right arm, cuts on the right side of the forehead and the left eyelid. The autopsy also disclosed that Cintron suffered a lacerated spleen from a blow that caused massive bleeding in the abdominal cavity. . . . There were also five fractures of four ribs and scattered small hemorrhages indicating a blow to the stomach."

McGrath told the press the knife story because that's what the guards told him; the commissioner did not speak to a single inmate about the incident.

James, Cruz, Smith, Butler, Waren, and Cintron are only

six citizens who died in city prisons in 1971. There are eleven more forgotten names, including Lavon Moore, who many believe was beaten to death by guards.

For months Commissioner McGrath has been explaining this body count by telling the press that the death toll in his prisons is no higher than in other large cities. But now statistics are available to suggest McGrath is in error. In the first eight months of 1971, no suicides were recorded in the prisons of Atlanta, Boston, or Dallas, while Philadelphia and Chicago have each had one. Cleveland hasn't had a prison suicide since 1963, and there have been no suicides in the prisons of Cincinnati, Houston, or Montgomery since 1969. St. Louis hasn't had one since 1968.

New York has had eleven suicides and seventeen deaths in its prisons in ten months.

New York's jails have a population of about 10,000. Houston has 2,200, Chicago 3,500, and Philadelphia 2,700. So in terms of percentage, New York City experiences far more deaths per 1,000 inmates than does any other major city.

The death rate may be the most gruesome proof of the city's failed system of corrections, but it is not the only evidence.

Health care, for example, is almost nonexistent. Most prison doctors are over sixty-five and accept the $15,000-a-year job because they can no longer handle a normal practice. According to ex-inmates I have talked to, the prison doctors sleep most of the time and become annoyed if a prisoner has an epileptic fit, or vomits, or screams from the agony of kicking heroin cold turkey. Often inmates are diagnosed incorrectly, given the wrong medication, and told they are faking if they complain of sickness.

In May, 1971, Councilman Carter Burden held a public hearing on health care in the prisons, which he called "scandalous at best." At that time Burden released an unpublished Health Services Administration study of medical care in the jails that found the average medical examination for an incoming inmate lasted two minutes and did not even include a test for venereal disease. The city report described prison doctors as "not adequate to their tasks." It also said that it took "four to six months" to order medicines and drugs, and that there was only one X-ray machine serving 10,000 inmates.

Dr. Michael Kondell appeared at the hearing to explain why he had quit the Correction Department in disgust after four months in the Rikers Island clinic. "I quit," he said, "because I became convinced it was impossible to practice adequate, humane medicine within the Department of Correction. . . . It was impossible, for example, for a doctor to order special medication twice a day for an inmate. No matter how sick the man was, the correction officers wouldn't give it to him because it broke up their routine. It was also impossible for me to order special diets for inmates. . . . I saw diabetic inmates rushed to Bellevue, where their conditions were stabilized, and then they were sent back to Rikers with the recommendation they be placed on a low carbohydrate diet. But that was never done because it was too much trouble."

Bill vanden Heuvel tells the story of how he noticed a

prisoner in the Tombs who had "a bloody hole in his scalp. He was also naked and gave off the most awful stink. So I went directly to the prison doctor to ask him to go see the man. But the next day I saw the prisoner again and no doctor had talked to him. Twice more that happened. I told the doctor to see this poor dazed guy on the eighth floor, and each time nothing happened. The fifth time—three weeks later—the doctor finally saw the guy and found out he had a lice condition so terrible that he had scratched a hole in his own head."

The absence of rehabilitation programs is another basic index of failure.

The city's whole criminal justice budget for 1970–71 was $843 million. Of this sum, the smallest part, 0.4 percent, was spent on what should be the largest job, prisoner rehabilitation programs like narcotics treatment, education, job training and placement, psychiatric care, and libraries. The 1971–72 Correction Department budget actually requested less money for rehabilitation programs ($3.2 million) than the previous year's budget ($3.5 million). The 1971–72 budget contains $200,000 for consultant fees and $2,000 for libraries.

In August, 1971, vanden Heuvel's watchdog agency released a study of the Rikers Island Reformatory that concluded:

The time has come to reform the reformatory. . . . Time and again recommendations have been made by the rehabilitative staff, but these reports have been lost in the phlegmatic bureaucracy of departments, commissions, bureaus, and boards who share responsibility for the city's adolescents. These reports have ended up on the desks of persons who either do not read or do not care. . . .

Little can be accomplished by just having a variety of programs on paper to which the inmates do not relate. . . . The Rikers Island Reformatory has become a warehouse to store problems for which the Department [of Correction] has no other easy resting place.

The report went on to say that it was "incomprehensible" that the reformatory has no narcotics programs, even though more than half the inmates are addicts, and that most of the inmates were "unaware" of whatever rehabilitation programs existed on paper. The vanden Heuvel study also pointed out that although 20 percent of the teenagers at Rikers were Spanish-speaking, the only program offered in Spanish was a Bible class.

It was in response to this report that Commissioner McGrath called the reformatory "one of the best facilities in the state, if not nationally."

The death rate, the foul medical care, the lack of rehabilitation programs are scandalous in themselves. But what makes it still worse is the attitude of Commissioner McGrath.

McGrath is a bureaucrat, a nice guy, a one-time reformer now desensitized by too many years on the job. McGrath just doesn't care anymore. He wants only to keep the lid on, ignore problems, take the guards' word about everything, and not bother the mayor, so the mayor won't notice him.

A good commissioner, like Patrick Murphy or Jerry

Kretchmer, is always pushing the mayor to try new things, to spend more money, to educate the public to an idea. McGrath never does that. He never fights for more funds or new programs. He was the only commissioner in 1971 who requested less money for his department than was actually appropriated. He takes no risks and never asks the mayor to do anything. And that is how he keeps his job and why he now has the longest tenure of any city commissioner. In fact, he is the only one of Lindsay's original commissioners still holding his job.

When the riot began in the Tombs on October 1, 1970, McGrath wasn't even in the city. He was in Philadelphia, where he had a consultant contract to advise that city on how to solve its corrections problems. McGrath was in Philadelphia ten days in 1970, and he was treated like a big shot there, like an expert penologist. It was nice. He didn't have to worry about the inmates of the Tombs not getting clean underwear, or Robert Cruz killing himself.

In March, 1971, when the Rankin report was published and named eighteen guards as guilty of using "excessive force" against inmates of the Queens jail, McGrath refused to suspend the guards. McGrath is a wise bureaucrat. He wants the correction officers' union on his side. McGrath knew the public storm would pass in a few days, and in the long run his job was safer if the union supported him. So these eighteen sadistic guards are still the law, and their victims are still the outlaws.

In May, 1971, McGrath testified before a committee of the City Council that things were getting better, that "the library in the Tombs is now open." But the library in the Tombs was not open. Robert Drake and Father Laurence

Gibney had both testified that the library was not open. It was a small, unnecessary lie, but McGrath felt compelled to say it in order to make the public image of his dreary dungeons a little better. And he got away with it.

These small episodes, I think, suggest the attitude that dominates the Correction Department under George Mc-Grath. And until this attitude changes, the jails will remain factories that manufacture crime, that turn muggers into murderers, because it is a system that brutalizes human nature.

The name "Correction" Department is a hoax. It is a "crime" department that corrects nobody and nothing.

September 2, 1971

POSTSCRIPT

In December of 1971, George McGrath was finally asked to resign by Mayor Lindsay. For a few months, McGrath was quietly kept on the city payroll as a "consultant." When that news became public, McGrath finally left town. He is now an administrator for the courts of Massachusetts. McGrath remains an advanced personification of the Peter Principle —an upward failure.

"Remember Attica"

THE MASSACRE at Attica was a classic situation for a Rockefeller. The inmates were mostly black and Puerto Rican, the poorest citizens of Bedford-Stuyvesant and the *barrio*. The hostages were low-income whites, with little education and less hope that their lives would improve. And above them all was one of the richest men on the face of the earth, holding the power of life and death in his hands.

It was not unlike other typical Rockefeller situations. For years he had been willing to see poor blacks and almost-poor whites die in Vietnam, while his own full life went on unaffected by the consequences. For years he has watched blacks struggle to win jobs in the construction trades, while Rockefeller, who has worn a hard hat only to campaign, profited from the political support of the bigoted building-trades unions. In the spring of 1971, when he wanted to cut the state's budget, Rockefeller sat in an air-conditioned room in Albany with four or five other rich Republicans and decided, over wine and steaks, that welfare payments should be reduced by 10 percent, that funds for narcotics programs should be cut by $35 million, and that anyone earning more than $4,500 a year should be cut from the Medicaid rolls.

So, in a sense, what Nelson Rockefeller did at Attica—

and what he refused to do—amounts to this: He stood safely behind an immense concentration of privilege and let the poor of both races kill each other.

During the four months preceding the September, 1971, riot, I had been corresponding with prisoners in Attica, and I had talked to several men recently paroled. The only conclusion one can come to is that inmates in Attica are treated worse than the animals in the Central Park Zoo. That's why in their thinking dying was equal to living.

All summer the inmates of Attica had spent fifteen and one-half hours of every day locked in their cells. Repeated petitions for more "yard time" were ignored. To spend fifteen and one-half hours "locked in" meant that the inmates left the yard at 3:30 P.M. on days when it was 100 degrees and were confined to their cells, in boredom and heat, till they went to sleep.

Inmates were permitted to shower only once a week. They were given clean underwear only once a week. Those who worked in the metal shop became stained and caked with thick grease, and they began to smell.

The food, one inmate wrote me, "contains dead bugs, pieces of glass, hairs, and we usually flush it right down the toilet. . . . I think the food they give us is so bad on purpose because there is a pig farm next to the jail, and they feed the pigs our garbage."

About 70 percent of the 2,400 inmates of Attica are black and Puerto Rican. Dozens speak only Spanish, knowing no English at all. But not one single guard in Attica is black or Puerto Rican, even though the prison is only thirty-five miles from Buffalo, where there are thousands of unemployed blacks and Puerto Ricans.

Custodial brutality appears to be commonplace in Attica. The guards all carry what they call "nigger sticks," according to inmates, and they use them at will.

There is no psychiatrist in Attica. The prison doctor, Paul Sternberg, stays behind a glass partition, rarely touches the inmates, and, through a microphone, often tells them they are faking.

There are no rehabilitation or education programs worthy of the name in Attica. For most of the inmates, the only work available is in the uncomfortably hot metal shop, for which they are paid twenty-five cents a day.

In contrast, while the inmates were in control they seem to have treated the hostages with more compassion than the guards had for them when they controlled the prison. When the shooting stopped, hostage Philip Watkins told reporters: "The prisoners addressed me as 'sir,' and offered me cigarettes, and they let the prison doctor set my arm. . . . When they [the inmates] ate hot meals, we [the hostages] ate hot meals. When they had sandwiches, so did we. And we had mattresses, and they didn't."

Two other hostages reported that at one point they were supposed to be executed. The inmates assigned to kill them, the hostages said, refused to do it and helped them fake it. "This wonderful Puerto Rican saved my life," hostage Elmer Huehn said. "He told me he didn't have the heart to do it."

It is my contention that forty-two men died at Attica because Nelson Rockefeller would not go to the prison and join in the negotiations. The committee of citizen negotiators asked Rockefeller to come. Congressman Herman Badillo, who was put on the committee by Rockefeller, personally pleaded with him by phone to come. The hostages gave interviews to television reporters begging Rockefeller to come. The families of the hostages sent the governor telegrams pleading for him to come. The previous October, when New York City experienced its prison riots, Mayor Lindsay agreed to meet with the prisoners and there was no loss of life.

Although Rockefeller would later suggest the revolt was the work of a few black revolutionaries, the evidence seems to be otherwise. The inmates at Attica had a list of demands long enough to cover two pages. Some of them were couched in the familiar rhetoric of Black Panther politics. Interestingly, though, one of the pages was specifically titled "Practical Demands." The demands for amnesty and for the removal of the warden—the very demands the state had decided were totally unacceptable—were *not* on that page. The distinction the prisoners themselves made between their "practical demands"—every one of which was related to actual prison conditions—and the others suggests that there was reason to keep the talks going, that there *was* some hope of avoiding bloodshed.

The committee of observers wanted to continue to negotiate. There was no reason not to wait a week, or even a month, before giving up all hope of a settlement. But Rockefeller was determined, out of pride, perhaps, or ambition, that he would not even talk to the inmates, despite the pleading of the hostages and the negotiators. He was able to decide coldly that men might have to die so that he might save face, appear tough, or defend some abstraction.

He was able to eat a good breakfast, have an 8:00 A.M. meeting with Dr. William Ronan, and make a decision that an undetermined number of lower-class people could die this day. Yet I wonder, would Rockefeller have so easily refused even to talk with the inmates if they had been holding Ronan hostage, or his own brother David? Why were forty-two lower-class lives not worth a one-hour flight to Attica?

A few hours after the massacre of the inmates and hostages, Rockefeller's office released a statement. Its first sentence read, "Our hearts go out to the families of the hostages who died in Attica." It pointedly had no sympathy for the mothers and children of the dead inmates. In fact, thirty-six hours after the deaths, desperate mothers and wives of Attica prisoners, too poor to go upstate, were still calling the Fortune Society because the state had not bothered to release the names of the thirty-two dead inmates.

Rockefeller's statement also tried to blame the uprising on "outside forces" and "revolutionary tactics of militants." Yet, his own correction commissioner, Russell Oswald, seemed to recognize the real cause of the rebellion when he immediately agreed to twenty-eight of the inmates' demands. But why should it have taken a riot in the first place for American citizens—convicted felons, to be sure, but still under the protection of law—to secure the right to "religious freedom" or "uncensored mail," "a limit on the time spent in solitary confinement" or "access to a dentist"?

The day after the Attica shoot-out, autopsies disclosed that the hostages did not die of cut throats, as the state had claimed, but of shotgun and rifle wounds. The prisoners had no guns. Only the police Rockefeller sent to storm the prison had them. And the state's description of mutilations also turned out to be a lie.

I don't know if what Rockefeller did in Attica is popular. I don't know whether a desire to impress the president played any role in Rockefeller's decision not to meet with the Attica inmates. It is quite possible, given Rockefeller's character, his enthusiasm for the Vietnam war, his support for legislation giving police the right to shoot looters, that the low value he places on human life could not be made any lower, even by his ambition for national office.

In any case, I pray Rockefeller is not forty-two corpses closer to the presidency. A century ago, the cry was "Remember the Alamo." Now, whenever Rockefeller shows himself in public, the cry should be "Remember Attica."

September 27, 1971

Parody
of Progress

THE NEW $25 million Women's House of Detention on Rikers Island stands as a monument to the folly of politicians and planners.

On the outside, it looks like the most beautiful prison in the world. It has modern dorms instead of cells; it is clean and well lighted, and filled with recreational and educational facilities. It is surrounded by fifty-five acres of space and trees. When Mayor Lindsay opened it on June 18, 1971, he said it was "the most modern, comprehensive detention and rehabilitation center in the nation."

But on the inside it is another story. Nothing works. Most of the rehabilitative programs do not exist because of a shortage of correction officers. The prison population is already forty over capacity. The classrooms, the gym, the library, the outdoor recreation area, the sewing room, and the beauty shop are all partially idle and empty. The health system is a horror. The commissary is badly stocked and overpriced. The prison itself is run on strict military regimentation. And it is badly located, so that it takes two hours and two fares to get there from Bed-Stuy. And so, despite the comfortable surroundings and glittering exterior, many of the inmates say they actually preferred the old, ugly, rat-filled women's jail in Greenwich Village.

The first two things a visitor to the new Women's House sees are portents of the absurdity to follow. One is a sign that says no visitor under sixteen is allowed, meaning that inmates can't see their own children, the cruelest possible punishment. The second thing a visitor sees is the first of many clocks in the institution: It has never been changed and runs constantly on daylight saving time. When I asked why, Captain Freeman said there were not enough guards to change it back. She explained that 210 correction officers were minimally required to staff the jail, and, since only 165 were now on duty, nothing was managed well.

"They spent $25 million to build this place, and then they didn't give us enough money to run it," the captain said. (The correction officers were all impressive and have submitted their own petition of grievances to the mayor.)

My tour guide through the jail, John Walsh of the Correction Department, was bright and candid, and he let me talk to anybody and see anything I wanted.

Our first stop was the small commissary. The women on line complained that fresh fruit and cold cream and Afro combs were unavailable. The prices struck me as outrageous: a quarter for cookies, ten cents for a stamped envelope, a nickle for a pencil, twelve cents for a bar of soap, a penny for a book of matches. Each inmate receives an allowance of $10 a week. Later I discovered through the Board of Correction that the commissary is actually run on a profit, that the stock is purchased wholesale and sold to the inmates above cost. The profit goes into a special fund, but no one seems to know who administers this fund or how much money is currently in it.

The first two inmates I talked to at random complained about the methadone detoxification program. One said it took thirty-six hours after her arrest to get her first dose of methadone, and by that time she was vomiting and kicking cold turkey. The second woman said she was afraid of methadone, didn't want it, would prefer to kick on her own, but she was being forced to take methadone.

Another inmate in the commissary tried to explain why she preferred the old Women's House. "You can't use any of the facilities here. I want to go to school, and they won't let me. I want to visit my friends, and they won't let me go to another floor. In the other place we would move around more. Here they don't let us go no place without a guard, even to the library. They got cops with guns outside, they got that river, we're on an island. I ain't going nowhere. And they think I'm going to escape. We get locked in our cells five hours a day. They count us five times every day, man."

Later, another woman in the cafeteria agreed that the infamous old women's jail had its advantages over the new one. "No one can visit me here. It's too remote. They don't allow no visiting on weekends. My people work during the week. In the Village, my people could talk to me from the street. This place is too far away from everything. Also, I have to talk to my husband through a glass window, through a telephone. We can't touch. . . . They are crazy about security here. They think I can swim across that big deep river out there."

The medical staff is straight out of a Dracula movie.

The prison psychiatrist is Dr. G (he asked that his name not be used). He is there only fifteen hours a week and is paid $15,000 a year. He seems like one of the more repressed human beings I have ever seen.

"Do you have any regular patients?" I asked.

"No, there is no time for that. Mostly I just medicate the girls. I can only see them for about five minutes. There are 700 girls here, remember."

"What kind of problems do they come to you with?"

"Oh, this morning I had one girl who was very upset. Her two codefendants had already gone home, and she was facing seven and a half to fifteen years."

"What did you tell her?"

"I told her not to act out so much."

"Couldn't you just tell her why she was still here and her codefendants on the outside?"

"Oh no. That's for the legal department to decide."

When I asked Dr. G why he kept referring to the inmates as "girls" rather than as "women," he replied, "They much prefer to be called girls—it makes them feel younger."

(In August of 1970, Dr. Violet Stephenson resigned as the director of psychiatry for the city's Correction Department. Dr. Stephenson, who was widely respected, said at the time that the mental health program in the jails was "disgracefully inadequate" and that the department "functions along military lines and is phobic about any program which represents change. . . . They don't let me help anybody.")

The physicians are even worse.

Dr. Belle Shedowitz is the head physician. When she saw

me and Benita Feurey of radio station WRVR she said, "Go away, I don't want to talk to any reporters." Then, pointing to Ms. Feurey's tape recorder, she said, "Get that camera out of here." Our tour guide, Mr. Walsh, then quietly took Dr. Shedowitz aside to persuade her to talk to us.

While that conversation was going on, Ms. Feurey noticed a memo posted on the wall of the infirmary. This is what it said: "Sanitary napkins are not to be issued indiscriminately due to severe plumbing stoppages. If this problem is not resolved it will be necessary to place strict controls on the issuance of sanitary napkins."

Mr. Walsh then returned and said Dr. Shedowitz and her three assistants would agree to an interview. The four women, all of them in their sixties and seventies, sat down at the head of a table.

Dr. Shedowitz admitted that no pregnancy test or Pap smear for cervical cancer is given to incoming inmates, although they all receive painful vaginal inspections after every court appearance in a search for "contraband" (probably heroin).

When I repeated to the doctor some of the many complaints I heard from inmates about medication and health care, she snapped: "Why do you believe only the inmates? Most of them are fakers, malingerers. They all come to us with phony complaints, looking for attention. If they complain every day, we know they are trying to trick us."

I then asked what the VD rate was among inmates.

"About 50 percent," she said.

"That sounds high," I suggested.

"Well, maybe it's 30 percent," she said.

At that point Mr. Walsh leaned over to me and said,

"Don't quote that figure. She doesn't know what she's talking about."

When Dr. Shedowitz admitted there was not one full-time gynecologist on the staff of the women's jail, the interview returned to the absence of a Pap test for cancer, which all women are urged to have annually.

"We only do a Pap smear," one of the other doctors said, "if there is some indication that it is necessary, if we find a lump or something down there."

It was explained that the smear was intended as a preventive technique, and if there was already "a lump," then the preventive function was lost.

"I don't understand what you're saying," said the doctor.

Later, when I talked to city officials and penologists, they all said the only sensible remedy for the wretched medical system in prisons would be affiliation contracts negotiated with medical schools and voluntary hospitals. Health Services Administrator Gordon Chase says he is already working on this and hopes the medical establishment responds affirmatively.

The story of the new women's prison is really a parody of the idea of progress.

The old dungeon on Greenwich Avenue was a hellhole. Community groups, ex-inmates, politicians admitted this. After years of agitation, ground was finally broken for the new Women's House on April 11, 1967. The city appropriated $25 million for the project.

The best engineers and architects were hired, the construction was completed in four years, and in June, 1971, the television cameras and the mayor came to Rikers Island for the official opening. It seemed to be a day of hope, a sign that government could actually accomplish something useful.

But the hope was false. It appears that almost nobody actually gets rehabilitated at the new prison. The good programs only work on paper. There is no money for staff—correction officers, doctors, psychiatrists, nurses. The prison is already overcrowded, the commissary is overpriced. And the mayor has not been back since he gave a superb speech about penal reform at the opening ceremonies.

From the outside, the new women's prison looks like a college dorm. On the inside it is a warehouse, where "the count" is the most important thing.

But it is still new, and the potential remains to make it a model prison. All it takes is a different attitude and a little money. Otherwise, the city will have spent four years and $25 million—only to make things worse.

December 2, 1971

POSTSCRIPT

The Dracula-like doctors described in this piece have been removed from the women's prison. They have been replaced by younger, more humane medical personnel, and a contract has been negotiated with Montefiore Hospital in the Bronx to provide improved health care to the women.

Budget and staff problems, however, persist, and some of the new prison facilities remain unused by the inmates.

Ghetto of Pain

SPOFFORD HOUSE is the detention center for seven- to sixteen-year-olds in the South Bronx. It has long been infamous for brutality, sadism, forced homosexuality, overcrowding, and corruption. When Assemblyman (now Congressman) Bert Podell went through it a few years ago, he wept.

There have been periodic public efforts to clean up Spofford House. In 1967 a series of *Post* columns by James Wechsler led to a full investigation. As a result the name was changed from Youth House to Spofford House. The responsibility for running it has been passed from a private board to the Family Court and the Department of Probation and then, since November, 1971, to the Human Resources Administration (HRA). A few improvements have been made. The overcrowding has ended, and there is a new infirmary. But in concept and administration, Spofford remains a warehouse to store hurt children.

In early 1971 I visited Spofford. I asked an eleven-year-old if there was a problem with drugs inside the place.

"Sure, man," he said, "we get all the dope we want in here."

"How?"

"The guy who drives us to court sells it to us. One fix for a carton of cigarettes. A set of works for two cartons."

Another kid, twelve or thirteen, told me there were a lot of rapes and forced homosexuality. The biggest perpetrator, he said, was a cook employed by the institution.

There were no functioning rehabilitation programs. There were complaints of beatings. Nothing was going on in the classrooms. Many of the children sat around all day just watching television. The eleven-year-olds were mixed together with the sixteen-year-olds. Many children had been there for six and nine months, although the legal limit for detention in Spofford is supposed to be forty-five days. Though most of the children were only truants or runaways, the place felt like an adult prison.

For several years the Institute for Juvenile Justice has been documenting the horrors of Spofford House. It was Larry Cole of the Institute who first directed James Wechsler's attention to the scandal in 1967. And it was Cole and Stu Black, also of the Institute, who arranged for my tour of the facility.

In March of 1971, Cole called a press conference to demand that Spofford be closed. At the same press conference, a thirteen-year-old boy named Jimmy, just released from Spofford, appeared with his mother and described the beatings and cruelty of the place.

In August, 1971, Stu Black announced that the Institute was filing suit in federal and state courts seeking the immediate and permanent closing of Spofford.

Throughout this history, through each bureaucratic change, from 1966 till today, one man has remained ac-

countable for much of the day-to-day running of Spofford—
Arthur Cole. In the files of old affidavits, clippings, memos,
and depositions, Cole's name keeps appearing, although he
has managed to avoid the media's focus.

A December 3, 1969, statement by Bernard Levine, the
United Federation of Teachers chapter chairman at Spofford:

I would suggest that the Director of the Department of Probation, John Wallace, and the Director of Operations at the Spofford Juvenile Center, Arthur Cole, are guilty of the grossest
forms of malfeasance and nonfeasance in that they have done
nothing to eliminate the deplorable conditions that exist, and
that in fact, many of their practices and policies are blatantly
contrary to the best interests of the youngsters who are placed
in their custody.

Excerpts from a statement by Lawrence Zuccolo, assistant principal of the school at Spofford:

One of the most important contributions of the public school
servicing the Juvenile Center has been the summer program. For
seven years, it has afforded a remedial program in reading and
arithmetic as well as some peripheral subjects. Under all previous program administrations, the program has been wholeheart-
edly welcomed. In the spring of 1969, the Board of Education
made its customary announcement that funds had been allocated
and 15 teaching positions assigned for the forthcoming summer. Surprisingly, the program was flatly rejected on the orders
of Mr. John Wallace, Mr. Wallace Nottage, and with the approval of Mr. Arthur Cole. One hundred forty to 150 boys were
thereby condemned to overcrowded dormitories with no recreational or educational programs.
Narcotics addicts have been indiscriminately mixed with the
general dormitory population. They are admitted to class where

their physical condition causes them to lay out over desks and chairs and on the floors. No education can take place for the other boys and no medical attention is administered to the addicts.

Over the past two years I have witnessed numerous brutal cases of physical abuse of boys forced into homosexual relations with other boys. Boys have suffered severe bruises, torn rectal areas of incapacitating degree, emotional and moral impairment. Many younger boys sent to sleep with older individuals have reported brutal beatings and forced acts of sexual perversion. One case brought to me by a Riverview teacher involved a youngster whose eyesight had been impaired by a brutal assault which involved a blow to his temple resulting in unconsciousness. He had not received any medical attention for about a week. I rushed this boy to the medical unit. A day or two later, it was discovered that the boy had suddenly been dismissed from the institution.

For approximately 1½ to two years after the Department of Probation takeover, there was only one social worker and no case aides to service approximately 450 to 500 youths. The old administration had numerous certificated social workers and approximately 14 case aides. Recently a few token case aides were hired. These are not social workers; they are largely interim employees with no background in this profession. There is still only one certificated social worker.

The administration, despite our and the dormitory supervisors' pleas, has failed to set up any standards of discipline or order. Boys who assault other boys or disrupt the school program are permitted to commit these acts with impunity. Personnel, as well as other youngsters, are constantly attacked and beaten.

Throughout the two years of Department of Probation administration, teachers have been harassed by the administration repeatedly. The morale of my teachers has fallen very badly.

Larry Cole and Stu Black recently showed ABC newscaster Edward P. Morgan through Spofford. (Morgan is also a board member of the Institute for Juvenile Justice.) It was the first time Cole and Black had been there since responsibility for running Spofford had been formally transferred to HRA, and they found out that Arthur Cole had been quietly appointed to be the number two man ("head of operations") in the new bureaucratic structure. Officially it is called the Special Services for Children Bureau with HRA.

On his "Shape of the News" network broadcast, Morgan talked about Spofford and concluded: "After a pledge of a clean sweep when the youth prison was taken from the Probation Department recently and given to the welfare administration [HRA], Arthur Cole mysteriously emerged as a special assistant to the new management. To stem juvenile delinquency, you've got to cure adult delinquency first."

Says Larry Cole: "Arthur Cole is only a symbol. Keeping him in a position of power during three different administrations of Spofford demoralizes those workers on the staff who really like kids. The best people on the staff believe that Cole represents the city's real attitude because he is the only thread of continuity. They don't believe there can be any reform as long as he has power."

Wayne Mucci of HRA is now in charge of Spofford for the city. He says that he is "looking into" the well-substantiated allegations about Cole and that "Mr. Cole came over from Probation as part of the transfer. He was director of operations. I had no say in it. But I will investigate all charges of previous wrong-doing."

Mucci also agrees with the Institute's objective of closing Spofford permanently. "It should never have been built," he says. "My goal is to get rid of it. We now have the money to develop alternative satellite facilities. We want to create 172 beds for kids in open settings. We have twenty foster homes authorized to take in two kids each. We have approval for group homes with house parents, hopefully young, married college couples. We plan to rent apartments and provide parent substitutes, psychiatrists, and social workers. And we have a federal grant for small residences around the city to house the kids."

The problem is neither policy nor funding, but "finding neighborhoods that are willing to accept these small facilities," according to Mucci.

"Look," he said, "the liberals in Greenwich Village won't let the overflow from the Tombs be put into the empty narcotics facility at 75 Morton Street with 500 beds. Our problem now is to find the communities that are decent enough to accept these local, decentralized alternatives to Spofford."

Spofford House is merely a symptom, the tip of an iceberg. It is the squalid dumping ground for the failures of the Family Court, broken ghetto families, the school system. It is a warehouse to store the children of poverty the rest of society wants to ignore. It does not heal or help any of the wounded children who pass through it. Spofford can only make them more bitter, more damaged.

The Family Court is a miserable example of turnstile justice. The children, often eight- and ten-year-olds, come before judges either unrepresented by counsel or with a Legal Aid lawyer who doesn't even know the kid's name; the case is disposed of in three minutes. Often the parents are not present. If a girl is promiscuous, or a boy has been in a fight, or a child has run away from home, he is sent to Spofford, she to Manaida. And there, he or she is placed in an environment of brutality, drugs, and forced homosexuality.

Closing Spofford seems an obvious imperative. What is a more basic requirement is a whole new system of juvenile justice: a more informal, humane substitute for the impersonal processing of the Family Court; homes and residences instead of detention centers; more citizen groups like the Institute for Juvenile Justice and fewer unaccountable bureaucracies skilled in buck-passing.

And what is most desperately needed is a generosity of character in this city that will embrace a foster home for juveniles, an auxiliary jail on Morton Street, a methadone program in South Brooklyn, and yes, a low-income housing project in Forest Hills.

As long as each separate neighborhood turns its back on the city's casualties, the great ghettos of pain—Brownsville, the Tombs, welfare hotels, and Spofford—will stand as monuments to man's worst instincts.

December 30, 1971

POSTSCRIPT

As a result of pressure generated from this article, Arthur Cole was removed from his responsibilities in connection with Spofford House. His new job, equally influential, is with the city's senior citizen program.

A month after this piece appeared, Wayne Mucci issued a press release declaring it was the city's new policy to close Spofford House within five years. Nothing, however, has been done yet to implement that policy goal. And the Civil Service employees' union has been lobbying against it, since they have more than 500 jobs at stake in keeping this particular hellhole open as a public facility.

Clinton Prison

"I haven't seen
the sun for a year"

HISTORY seems to remember its cruelest cultures by their prisons: the Nazis by Auschwitz, Stalin by his Siberian labor camps, the French by the Bastille, the British by their internment camps in Ulster, South Vietnam by its tiger cages. Modern America has contributed Attica, San Quentin, and now Clinton Prison in Dannemora, New York, to this awful litany.

For eight hours of one shattering day, I toured Clinton Prison with Assemblyman Tony Olivieri and David Rothenberg of the Fortune Society.

At first it was hard to absorb what I was seeing. Some of the guards seemed like decent and troubled men. Some of the inmates had only the normal complaints about food, doctors, and the Parole Board. I tried to keep in mind that these men were, after all, criminals with victims. I tried to see it through the eyes of the best guards.

It was only after we left that reality started to sink in. While most of the prison functions normally, about fifty men are locked in solitary confinement, in filthy five-by-seven cages, some for as long as eleven months without the world's notice, without a hearing, without hope the warden, or the legislature, or the governor, or the Supreme Court will intervene. These fifty men are enduring, in anonymity, conditions that if ever filmed and put on television, like Willowbrook, would shame a civilized nation. But cameras and tape recorders are not allowed in Clinton.

The inmates are alone twenty-four hours of every day. They can't see each other. They eat, shit, and sleep in their cells. Many have had their law books, legal papers, and personal possessions taken from them. Their five-by-seven cages have no tables, no light bulbs, no chairs. Several of the men have no mattresses and sleep on the concrete floor; several of them have no toilet, and have to make do with a bucket which is emptied once a week. If they want to shower once a week, they are forced to go out through the back of their cells, outdoors into the deep snow and zero cold. They could just as easily reach the showers through an indoor route. They get no outdoor recreation and no medical attention. The cells stink from shit, vomit, and sweat, and the inmates have no mops to clean them. Their mail is opened and censored. Their shouted conversations are tape-recorded by the guards and the tapes filed in the warden's office. The inmates believe their food is laced with Thorazine, which causes them to fall into a stupor. When they have protested these conditions, they have been tear-gassed and beaten. Their being placed in segregation has ended any chance they might have of parole.

The men in solitary in Clinton were assembled there during three separate roundups of inmates made over the last eleven months, including one the night of the Attica uprising. On these occasions, any prisoner suspected of being a "militant" or "political" was removed from the general prison population, handcuffed, and put in solitary. No hearings, no appeals, no reasons.

When a lawyer asked Clinton's warden, J. Edwin Lavallee, how he could tell who was a "militant," the warden replied, "One way we tell is if he signs his letters 'Right on.' "

When I asked a guard how he could spot a troublemaker, he said: "I look into their cells. If they have certain books, certain newspapers, I know he's trying to overthrow the system here."

Many of the men locked in solitary, however, are not revolutionaries. They write to lawyers with Legal Aid, the ACLU, and the Fortune Society. They want to read the *Amsterdam News* and *The Village Voice*. They address appeals to Assemblyman Arthur Eve of Buffalo and Congresswoman Bella Abzug. They do not use the rhetoric of the Panthers. They do not think of themselves as political prisoners; not one of the dozen men I talked to claimed he was innocent of his original crime. All they say, again and again, is "We are human beings, not animals."

In northern New York state, prisons play the role army oases and military installations play in the South. Attica, Auburn, and Clinton are props for the economy, a taxpayers' subsidy providing hundreds of jobs in white rural areas.

The population of Clinton Prison is urban poor—about 75 percent black and Puerto Rican. But there is not a single black guard, and the one Spanish-speaking guard seems to be especially distrusted by the inmates.

Like Attica, the inaccessibility of the prison makes it very hard for the inmates to be visited by their families and friends. The round-trip bus fare from Harlem or Bed-Stuy to Plattsburg is $26, and the trip takes more than six hours. From Plattsburg, a visitor must still take a taxi (for $5) to the prison in Dannemora. It is impossible to make the trip in a single day. So visitors must stay overnight in Dannemora, paying for food and accommodation; more than likely, this means a second day off from work. One young inmate whom David Rothenberg visited had not received a single visit in three years and was almost in tears when David asked to see him.

The remote location of the prison—about thirty-five miles from the Canadian border—also discourages outside scrutiny. Olivieri was the first legislator from New York City to see Clinton this year, and I was the first journalist. Harlem State Senator Sidney von Luther recently held a press conference attacking conditions at Clinton and claiming to have been "rudely treated by guards," but according to both the warden and the prisoners, he had actually never visited the prison. And his charge of overcrowding was also false. There are about 200 empty cells.

(It seems absurd to watch fifty reporters follow Clifford Irving around the city, recording his "no comments," while the conditions at Clinton go unreported. Of course, if Clinton explodes like Attica, they'll be there—after the fact—blaming William Kunstler or someone else for the tragedy. It is the neglect of the "ordinary" that is the media's weakness in covering the criminal justice system.)

Also like Attica, the prison serves the inmates so much pork because there are several large pig farms in the area, and this is a further prop for the upstate economy. The day we visited, a fatty bacon was the main dish for lunch. There are about a hundred Muslim inmates, and they refuse on religious grounds to eat any pork. Most of the other inmates didn't eat it because it tasted terrible and because they get so much of it they can't stand it any more.

Ralph Mercado is twenty-two years old, serving a one- to three-year sentence for robbery. He was a member of the Young Lords.

"I came here from the Elmira reformatory in April, 1971," he told us. "They immediately put me in segregation, for no reason. A few months ago they let me out for a few weeks. They took pictures of me. They watched me. The hacks walk around with tape recorders. On January 14 of this year they put me back in the hole. They also put into solitary anyone who was my friend, anyone I talked to while I was in the general population, cats who aren't even political.

"It's hell in here, man. The hacks drop your food sometimes on the floor and say they are sorry if they know you're hungry. They call us nigger and spic. At night, when it's below zero, they open up the windows, and I don't even have a blanket. They put drugs in our food, and suddenly there's no rapping on the tier for two days because we're all asleep. They've taken away all my good time [time off for good behavior]. But I get out on May 19, 1973."

Casper Gary has been in solitary for more than six months. He is back in Clinton for parole violation after serving thirteen years.*

"They rip up our legal papers, they intercept letters from

* Casper Gary is now out and working in Manhattan.

our lawyers sometimes and throw them away. Not all the time, just sometimes, so we never know. But I have a friend who works out front with the trash, and he sees the lawyers' mail torn up."

Essex Ray we could only see in handcuffs—"for your protection," we were told. He has been in solitary for almost a year. He was a leader of the Auburn uprising in November, 1970. He is underweight and very tense, his eyes bulging out of his sallow face.

"Last June 25, they beat us all. They beat us with bats and pick handles. Then they gassed us in our cells. They poured hot water on us. They are trying to kill us, to drive us mad. They are tape-recording everything we say."

(Warden Lavallee admitted in a letter to Congresswoman Abzug: "We do have tape recorders, and they are used in Unit 14 to record conversations relative to planning of riots, revolts against the government of the United States, and for violation of rules of Department of Correction Facilities.")

James Cunningham is twenty years old. He was put in segregation as part of the roundup of January 14, 1972.

"I'm locked up twenty-four hours a day. They don't let me read none of the books I get sent—Malcolm X, George Jackson. The only books they let you read are Nick Carter murder mysteries. They show us movies here about killing the Indians. But I can't even read *The Village Voice*."

Jimmy Hughes is twenty-six and a high school graduate. He has been in solitary since Attica.

"There is only one way we can get out of segregation. They want us to sign some paper that says we won't talk about conditions in here and that we will obey the rules and regulations. Shit, we have to obey the rules anyway.

"When I asked them why I was being put in segregation, they told me it was because I had a friend in Attica. I'm locked up all day. They don't let me participate in no classes, no programs, no rehabilitation. I'm willing to do my time, but they're trying to make me commit suicide. They keep saying I'm preaching revolution. They even put some white guys in the box, for nothing, for just talking in the yard. I'm trying to be cool, but it's something else, man, being locked up alone for six months for no reason. I'm not a revolutionary. But I'm not an animal. I'm a man."

Robert X. Smith is forty-two years old. He was a close associate of the late Malcolm X. He is now quite sick. He has been in the prison hospital five times in the last four months. He has a gastric ulcer and hypertension. He is not now in solitary, but is under constant surveillance and harassment by the guards.

"I was in solitary, but I got sick. They took away my milk. I need it for my health. . . . I think the administration here is trying to provoke us. They want tension, an incident, so they can hire more guards, so they can pay more overtime. . . .

"On January 14, they threw me into solitary. I asked why, and they said it was for the smooth running of the institution. I never was given a hearing. They say I'm a leader because I was once associated with the late Minister Malcolm. . . . I subscribe to the *Amsterdam News* and the Fortune newspaper, but they don't let me get it. When I get visitors, they don't let them see me. They keep feeding me all the worst foods for my ulcer. . . . But the basic thing here is that they *want* another Attica. Ever since Rockefeller cut the budget, they've been trying to stir us up with all these beatings and roundups. . . . I'll be okay, but I worry about some of those guys in solitary for nine months. They may try and kill themselves."

Raziel Arziel has been locked in solitary for eleven months. He has no shoes or mattress in his cell. When he saw us, he started to make a speech that lasted for about fifteen minutes. He began by showing us a metal bucket filled with shit.

"I don't have a sink or a toilet. I have to defecate in this. Sometimes they take it away and I defecate on the floor. Then I have to eat on the floor, next to the shit. I've been denied access to the library, to everything in this prison. . . . I haven't seen the sun for a year.

"The goon squads beat us regularly. On Sunday, July 11, at 10 A.M., they beat us with baseball bats and gassed us. On June 25, at noon, they beat us. I saw brother Robert Clarke beaten unconscious by fifteen goons right in front of my cell. . . .

"They're trying to make us crazy. They tape everything we say. One night they played it back to us over the PA system. . . . Every time we see a lawyer they give us a strip search, they search our rectum and our genitals. It's degrading. They do it so we don't want to see our lawyers. Once when I went to see my lawyer they came into my cell and took all my legal papers. Once when I came back I saw an electric wire because they had put a secret microphone into my cell. They're trying to make us into vegetables with drugs in food. . . ."

At the end of the day we met with eight guards for about a half hour. What do you guys want, Olivieri asked, more money? Better training?

They all shouted out no, what we want is a separate prison—the maximum-maximum-security prison—for "political incorrigibles" and "militants."

"Troublemakers should not be allowed to mix with the rest of the prison population," one guard said. "They cause riots."

February 17, 1972

POSTSCRIPT

Clinton remains the most brutal prison I have experienced.

In June of 1973, I visited Greenhaven Prison and saw two men I had interviewed at Clinton—Robert 35X Smith and Roger Whitfield. They told me more horror stories of Clinton and said Greenhaven was "paradise" in comparison.

Smith said he had requested permission to start a Muslim mosque in Clinton, but was told by Warden Lavallee that he, Lavallee, was "God" and that Smith must kiss his feet.

At Greenhaven, Smith was able to organize a mosque with little difficulty. Greenhaven also has an inmate newspaper, a black deputy warden, a class in Italian culture, and nothing equivalent to Clinton's Unit 14.

Clinton continues to hold more than thirty inmates in solitary without a hearing. During June of 1973, two inmates in solitary at Clinton died. Inmates claim the deaths were suspicious. Warden Lavallee would not comment on the deaths or even confirm they occurred.

"I am Attica"

Brother Herb, a veteran of the revolt in the infamous Tombs, is holding the single small microphone in the glare of a flood lamp; like most of the inmates he is wearing a prison blanket cut like a poncho. Bull-shouldered and hoarse, with the remarkable eloquence that characterizes most of the inmate speakers, Herb has told the visitors in an earlier daylight visit: "I am Attica."

Now, laying down the prisoners' demands to loud cheering and shouts of "Right on!," Herb is skillfully heightening his brothers' morale; what the visitors are hearing, he says, is "but the sound before the fury of those who are oppressed. When you are the anvil, you bend, but when you are the hammer you strike."

—Tom Wicker,
The New York Times,
September 14, 1971

A MONG the 200,000 prison inmates in the United States, Brother Herb is a legend. When the filthy, overcrowded Tombs erupted in 1970, the inmates picked Brother Herb to escort the hostages to freedom and negotiate with Mayor Lindsay for their demands. When the 1,200 citizens of D block at Attica took over the yard in September, 1971, they elected Brother Herb to be their spokesman. When Manhattan District Attorney Frank Hogan indicted seven men for "leading" the Tombs riot, Brother Herb was one of them. When George Jackson's mother came to New York, the first person she asked to see was Brother Herb.

Brother Herb is Herbert X. Blyden, who describes himself as "a Muslim, a socialist, and a Leo." But Blyden is not unique. There are hundreds of Blydens in America's prisons —black, furious, eloquent, and probably doomed. Walk into any prison yard and in the sea of young black faces there will be Blydens and George Jacksons among them. Blyden at thirty-five is not very different from Elliott Barkley, who died in the Attica massacre at the age of twenty-one. Barkley, in Attica only for violation of parole, was a brilliant leader among the inmates. Today, nobody even remembers his name. The Harlem Four became wise men during the eight years they were held without bail in the Tombs. Folsom Prison has produced more important black writers —George Jackson, Larry West, Eldridge Cleaver—than has the New York City public school system. So I write about Brother Herb only because I know him and I know his story. He is not some special mutation. He is a representative product of our courts and prisons.

Brother Herb is an impressive man—six feet, 205 pounds. His manner is dignified, almost formal, coupled with a sense of great power not used. His career in the Virgin Islands school system was over at the age of fourteen, but he has read all of B. F. Skinner and Hermann Hesse. He's an enthusiastic advocate of feminist liberation and the gay-rights movement. (Blyden himself is not gay.) A Muslim, he has never taken hard drugs. He loves music, especially Carole King and James Taylor. ("That song 'Fire and Rain'—it's about my life, man.") He reads *The Law Journal* every day and has developed a sophisticated knowledge of the law reminiscent of Lenny Bruce's.

Because his mind is so active, Blyden doesn't do time very well. He gets moody and depressed for long periods, and sometimes he talks about his own death. "I just can't adjust to prison," he says. "The anxiety, the noise, the celibacy, the lack of sleep, knowing I'm innocent—it all drives me crazy." He depends on music and a rich fantasy life to ease the maddening monotony of endless time in limited space.

But it is not, finally, Blyden's intelligence or his personality that is significant. It is his actual experience inside the system of criminal justice that is the story worth telling. It is a case history that suggests there is one law in this country for the powerful—for ITT and the president's friends in San Diego—and another law for the powerless—for Herb Blyden, the Harlem Four, and the 500 men who are in the Tombs tonight for no other reason than they are men of so little property that they can't raise $100 cash bail.

On August 19, 1965, Blyden was arrested by New York City police on a charge of armed robbery. He is now serving a fifteen- to twenty-year sentence on that charge, although there is substantial evidence that he is innocent.

Blyden was accused of participating in the stickup of an Alexander's Rent-a-Car agent at 903 Sheridan Avenue in the Bronx. The robbery netted $600. Blyden was charged with driving the getaway car. The actual gunman was never caught, and the money was never recovered.

At the time of his arrest Blyden was on welfare and living with his girl friend, Greta Jude, although he was not divorced from his wife. He was too poor to hire a lawyer; the court assigned him a Legal Aid Society attorney, Arthur Guff, who spent only a few minutes with Blyden before his trial. Overworked, Guff had no time to interview witnesses or prepare a defense. A reading of the trial transcript suggests that Guff did not even know the basic facts of the case. Blyden swore to him he was innocent; Guff told Blyden to plead guilty and hope to cop a plea for one and a half to five years.

Blyden's trial began in the Bronx on November 3, 1965. There was only one witness against Blyden, a gas station attendant named Dominick Maffucci, who testified he saw the driver of the getaway car "maybe four or five seconds . . . from the side but not the front. . . . He was colored and had a goatee."

On the afternoon of Blyden's arrest, Maffucci went to the 42d Precinct and the police allowed him to view Blyden through a one-way mirror—Blyden couldn't see him but Maffucci could see Blyden. Blyden was being questioned by two detectives. Maffucci said Blyden was the guy in the car.

On the witness stand Maffucci identified Blyden as the "colored guy with a goatee."

On cross-examination Maffucci admitted, "I didn't observe, I mean, I don't remember, actually, to tell the truth, I don't remember whether it was a full beard or what."

No other evidence was presented by the state identifying Blyden or placing him at the scene of the robbery. Blyden's black girl friend, Greta Jude, testified he was with her at the time of the robbery. An all-white jury—although Bronx County was 35 percent black and Puerto Rican at the time —convicted Blyden. The judge gave him fifteen to twenty years—the maximum.

The sentence was so stiff because it was Blyden's second offense. Eight years before, when he was twenty, Blyden stole $96 from a gas station that was partly owned by his father and where he worked part time. ("I did it. I was stupid.") His court-appointed lawyer at the time (who is now a judge) advised him to plead guilty, that he would be treated as a youthful offender and paroled. Instead, the judge sentenced Blyden as an adult to five years in the Elmira reformatory. With this on his record, Blyden was given the maximum in 1965.

This spring I visited Dominick Maffucci, who now owns a garage on Sherman Avenue, only a few blocks from the Bronx House of Detention. During our twenty-minute conversation Maffucci contradicted most of the original facts he testified to at Blyden's trial.

He claimed he observed Blyden for "fifteen minutes," not four or five seconds. He described Blyden as "140, no 160 pounds; no, make that 170 pounds." Blyden weighed over 200 pounds in 1965. Maffucci said he identified Blyden by recalling the license plate number of his car; he never mentioned the license plate during the trial. Maffucci also said he picked Blyden out of a lineup with "five or six other colored guys." Blyden says he was never in a lineup. Police records back him up.

I asked Maffucci what made him notice Blyden that hot August afternoon in 1965. "I always notice colored guys when they're just hanging around," he replied. "You never know when they're going to pull a knife on you, or something. I've helped the police catch a lot of the colored muggers. Blyden isn't the only one. I help the cops a lot."

A petition for a writ of habeas corpus in this case is now before Judge Dudley Bonsal. The writ argues that Blyden was denied due process by the "unnecessarily suggestive" one-man show-up and that he was denied effective counsel.

In October of 1970 there were 1,450 men jammed into 875 cells in the Men's House of Detention on White Street in Manhattan. Among them was Blyden, whose presence in the Tombs that week was an accident of history. Attica had been Blyden's graduate school. He had begun to read voluminously—everything from Marx to Marcus Garvey. He studied law and began to write his own briefs and petitions. He happened to be down from Attica because one of his handwritten appeals was due for a hearing in court. Complaints of brutality by guards were increasing. Men were waiting eight, ten, and twelve months for trials. The food had glass and hairs in it. The doctors were indifferent to inmate complaints of pain and sickness. The junkies were kicking cold turkey in their overcrowded cells. On October 1 a riot exploded spontaneously. It ended on October 5 when the inmates voted to release eighteen hostages in exchange for an immediate meeting with Mayor Lindsay. Blyden helped escort the hostages to safety and was chosen to be one of eleven prisoner-negotiators to meet with Lindsay to discuss grievances. This is how Blyden recalls the 2:00 A.M. meeting with the mayor:

"We wanted the press there to see what promises Lindsay made to us. But no reporters were allowed in. There was not even a stenographer present. Lindsay was Lindsay. Lots of promises and lots of rhetoric. I tried to explain that our problem was not the correction officers, but the system—the judicial system, the Legal Aid lawyers who tell us to plead guilty without asking if we are guilty, the bail system, the long wait for trials. . . .

"Then we asked Lindsay for a promise of no reprisals. He tried to pass the buck to McGrath and McGrath tried to pass it back to Lindsay. McGrath wouldn't give it. But the warden promised no physical reprisals, and he kept his word. There never were any beatings in the Tombs. At the end Lindsay finally guaranteed us no reprisals."

But in January of 1971 there was reprisal. Blyden and six other inmates were indicted on fifty separate counts of first-degree kidnapping. They were indicted even though none of the hostages were hurt and even though almost no one disputed the legitimacy of their demands.

There was a strange scene in the courtroom—Part 30 at 100 Centre Street—when the Tombs indictments were announced. First, the story was already on the street in the New York *Post,* even though grand jury proceedings are supposed to be secret. And second, Al Castro, the press aide to Correction Commissioner McGrath, was in the courtroom, feeding background information on the seven defendants to reporters. Again, this seemed a violation of the traditional separation of the DA's office from the Correction Department.

Hundreds of inmates participated in the revolt. No one has ever suggested the revolt was planned in advance. How, then, could seven men be singled out for such heavy indictments? Why was Blyden indicted?

The full answer will have to wait until the trial, but clearly involved is the dubious obsession of Frank Hogan, Manhattan's district attorney, with locking up militant blacks. The Panther Thirteen were rounded up, jailed for two years on unattainable bail, tried on bombing conspiracy indictments, and then acquitted. The Harlem Four were incarcerated for eight years and put through three trials before finally being granted lower bail over Hogan's objections. Prosecutors in Brooklyn and Queens are not prosecuting inmates who rioted in jails in those boroughs at the same time the Tombs uprising occurred. District Attorneys Thomas Mackell and Eugene Gold have dropped, or plea-bargained, all charges against the thirty-five inmates indicted on charges similar to those against the Tombs Seven. Only Hogan's office has insisted on bringing rebel inmates to trial.

This shows as well as anything the arbitrary and capricious nature of the law. Blyden faces 115 years for the Tombs riot because it occurred in Manhattan, while the inmates who rebelled in Queens face no added time. This is why no one can convince the Blydens of this world that the law is even rational, much less fair.

Clearly, the city's correction bureaucracy has it in for Blyden. Commissioner McGrath has talked openly—to Bill vanden Heuvel, the mayor's prison watchdog, as well as to his own staff—of his personal dislike of Blyden as an agitator and troublemaker. And Mike Dontzin, the mayor's assistant for correction, seems to hold a special grudge against Blyden. I have visited Blyden frequently at the Bronx House of Detention. One morning I was told I couldn't see him because there was a "strip search" of every prisoner going on. As I was about to leave, Dontzin and Bronx District Attorney Burton Roberts appeared. Dontzin, who knew I was friendly with Blyden, greeted me by saying: "Your buddy is trying to start a riot in this place. Why don't you wise up and realize that he's a dangerous psycho, a lunatic?"

The next day I came back to see Blyden and told Deputy Warden Charles Clark what Dontzin had said. Clark replied: "That's not true. Blyden had nothing to do with what happened yesterday. He's in segregation. He doesn't go anywhere without an officer. He hasn't caused us any trouble."

Blyden was indicted for the Tombs riot in January of 1971. Fifteen months later, he is still waiting for his trial to start. And the Tombs is still choked to 141 percent of capacity.

They call Attica "the end of the line." It is a huge maximum-security penitentiary thirty-five miles from Buffalo. While whites tend to be sentenced to Walkill Prison, blacks and Puerto Ricans always seem to end up in Attica and Clinton. On the day the Attica uprising began, the prison population was 65 percent black and Puerto Rican, but there was not one black or Puerto Rican guard.

By all accounts Brother Herb was working in the prison metal shop when the riot broke out on September 9. It was the white radical Sam Melville, who died in the troopers' attack, who first suggested that Blyden be made a member of the inmate negotiating committee as a representative of B Block. Blyden at first declined, but later he was elected chairman of the full committee that consisted of two spokesmen from each of the four blocks. In the yard Blyden was crucial in getting the four blocks together and in helping to forge the remarkable unity among black, white, and Puerto Rican inmates that prevailed during the uprising.

David Rothenberg of the Fortune Society was a member of the observers' committee; he remembers Blyden's conduct during the five days the inmates controlled the yard: "It was the last night, maybe ten hours before the massacre. Things were very tense during a mass meeting in the yard. One member of our observers' committee—not Kunstler—made a very inflammatory speech, a really violent speech. And I remember Blyden taking the microphone away from him and shouting, 'That's bullshit! I don't want to die. I want to live with dignity.' He shut the guy up, and there was a great cheer from the inmates. Blyden was very constructive."

At first Blyden didn't want to talk about the massacre at Attica that killed forty-two men. "It's too depressing," he said. But one rainy morning he opened up and the memories poured out.

"The guy standing to my left was shot and killed, and the guy standing just to my right was also killed. It all happened so fast it was unreal. It was eerie. The mist and gas came over everything, and then the helicopters, and suddenly the troopers came in shooting. One trooper grabbed me and said they would save me for the electric chair."

"What happened after the prison was recaptured?"

"Oh, we were beaten. They called us 'nigger' and made us crawl naked on the ground across the whole yard. Guys were vomiting and going into convulsions, and if they moved, they were beaten. Three inmates were murdered by the troopers after we gave up. They killed Sam Melville, Elliott Barkley, and Tom Hicks in the yard. Someday we will prove that. . . .

"Then after we crawled across the yard we had to run a gauntlet of about forty correction officers. We were still naked and they beat us with sticks and batons. Some guys had lighted cigarettes put against their genitals.

"When I got back to my cell I found out the guards had destroyed all my possessions. I was writing a book about the Tombs. I had written 300 pages in longhand. That was gone. I had all my legal papers in the cell, all my research for my appeal on the Bronx case, and that was gone. They even took away my eyeglasses and false teeth. They took everything I had. And every night the guards would come by my cell and tell me I was going to die. The guards would wake me up in the middle of the night to make these threats. And for about three weeks after the riot all they fed us was pork. They knew that as Muslims most of us couldn't eat pork."

A grand jury has been meeting in Wyoming County (Attica) for five months. The jury is all white, and most of its twenty-three members have families or friends who work in Attica Prison. The prison is as important to the economy of Wyoming County as, say, Fort Jackson is to the economy of Columbia, South Carolina.

I have talked to people who have testified before this grand jury. They report the jury isn't interested in why the governor ordered the troopers in with guns blazing. Or why it took 450 rounds of ammunition to subdue the prisoners. Or why fifteen unauthorized correction officers joined the attack and were responsible for at least two inmate deaths. Or why the troopers used dumdum bullets, outlawed by the Geneva Convention. Or why according to the Goldman Commission, which Rockefeller set up to probe Attica, 315 inmates were injured as a result of beatings by guards and troopers after the prison had been recaptured. Or who was responsible for the false story given the media, after the shooting stopped, that the hostages' throats had been slit by inmates, when, in fact, the hostages had been killed by the governor's own troopers.

Instead, almost all of the jury's questions have been about the inmate leaders and William Kunstler. Witnesses have been shown photos of Blyden and have asked questions about him. Once again justice seems intent on indicting the victim and exonerating the executioner.

So Brother Herb waits in a cell in the Bronx, waits for Judge Bonsal to rule on his habeas corpus writ, waits for Frank Hogan to begin his Tombs trial, waits for the Wyoming County grand jury to complete its deliberations. I'm white and middle class, and I would not want my life or liberty in the hands of these people.

May 15, 1972

POSTSCRIPT

In the fall of 1972, three of Blyden's codefendants in the Tombs case were brought to trial by Manhattan District Attorney Frank Hogan. A jury acquitted the three, and Hogan, in an extraordinary outburst, released a press statement attacking the jury's verdict.

Two months later, Hogan attempted to bring Blyden to trial on the same charges for which his codefendants were acquitted. But Justice Xavier Riccobono dismissed the case.

On September 1, 1973, Blyden was given a five-day furlough from Greenhaven Prison. Such a furlough seemed a sure portent of an imminent parole.

We had a party for Blyden. There were emotional toasts to Herb's future freedom after nine years in prison. Blyden also received a commitment for a job from the Urban League when he got out on parole.

On September 6, Blyden returned to Greenhaven. The next day he was indicted for homicide during the Attica riot by the Wyoming County grand jury.

Anniversary
for Attica

LLIOTT BARKLEY died a year ago today. He died in the yard of D Block at Attica. Barkley was twenty-one years old and black. He was in Attica for violation of parole. He had violated parole by being unemployed, and he was unemployed because he was fired when his boss discovered he was an ex-con.

A year ago today, Walter Dunbar, the deputy commissioner of corrections, stood outside the gray, thirty-foot wall of Attica and informed the media that inmates had murdered nine hostages by slitting their throats and that one hostage was castrated, his testicles stuffed in his mouth. Dunbar said the storming of the prison was "an efficient, affirmative police action."

A year ago today Nelson Rockefeller released a statement from his home on Fifth Avenue that began, "Our hearts go out to the families of the hostages who died at Attica." He pointedly offered no sympathy to Elliott Barkley's mother, living in Rochester's black ghetto, or to the children and widows of the twenty-nine inmates who died by his decision.

It is now a year later, the picture has slowly emerged, and I think it is clear who should be punished.

Every hostage who died on September 13, 1971, was killed by state police guns. The official version of slit throats and castration was disproved by the autopsies. We now know, thanks to the McKay Commission hearings, that between fourteen and seventeen correction officers, without permission, fired into the yard of D Block with their own hunting guns and that they killed two inmates. We now know that the state police were firing dumdum bullets, which are outlawed under international law and the Geneva Convention. We now know that 450 rounds of ammunition were fired into the yard in that "efficient" action, hitting one out of every ten inmates. We now know the inmates had no guns and fired no bullets. We now know, after a public screening of the official film of the police assault, that the first warning to the inmates to surrender came after four minutes and twenty seconds of heavy shooting. We now know it wasn't only the inmates and the hostages and the observers' committee who pleaded with the governor to come to Attica, but Correction Commissioner Russell Oswald on three separate occasions also implored the governor to come.

There is now also sufficient evidence to suggest another factor in the Attica massacre not mentioned by Governor Rockefeller or Commissioner Dunbar. That factor is racism.

On September 13, 1971, 65 percent of the 2,254 men in Attica were blacks and Puerto Ricans; whites somehow end up in nice prisons like Walkill. But not one of the guards at Attica was black or Puerto Rican. And not one of the 2,800 residents of the town of Attica was nonwhite. The guards in Attica called their batons "nigger sticks."

Of the 600 state police who stormed Attica, not one was black. When they surged into the yard, they were chanting, "White power, white power."

The racism even extended beyond death. In the Attica morgue, the dead guards were tagged with their names. The dead inmates were tagged, "P-1," "P-2," and so on.

Conditions inside Attica today are worse than before the riot. Most of the twenty-eight inmate demands that Commissioner Oswald quickly agreed to and admitted were "long overdue" have still not been implemented. There is still no narcotics program for inmates, the food is still served with glass, bugs, and hair in it, there are still frequent prisoner complaints of brutality and race-baiting by guards.

More than eighty Attica inmates, presumed "militants," have been locked in solitary confinement in other upstate prisons for the past 365 days. Twenty are still held in Attica's isolation unit. The men are in six-by-eight cages that have no chairs, no mirrors, no desks. The windows in their cells have been painted over and the cells are arranged so the men cannot see each other. They are permitted to exercise ten minutes a day and are granted one three-minute shower a week. Some have lost as much as fifty pounds. And they have not been formally charged with anything or given a hearing.

One of the most deeply felt of the twenty-eight demands was the removal of the two prison doctors, Sternberg and Williams. They are still there. One inmate in isolation went to Dr. Williams with severe chest pains. He was refused medication and told, "You should have died in the yard, nigger." Another inmate has a chronic bone infection in his leg. For months he was denied antibiotics and given twenty aspirins a day. He will soon have his leg amputated.

Attica was not unique in our recent history. Several times we have watched the state kill and the killers receive the special amnesty of the powerful. At the Algiers Motel, at Orangeburg, at Kent State, at Jackson State, the law acted as an outlaw and escaped accountability.

On this first anniversary of Attica, I meditate on the short life of Elliott Barkley, and I know that Nelson Rockefeller will never be held to account.

September 13, 1972

POSTSCRIPT

A week after this was written, the final report of the McKay Commission was published. The commission had been created by Governor Rockefeller immediately following the events at Attica. Its membership included Yale Law School Dean Burke Marshall and New York University Law School Dean Robert McKay. The members had been named by the chief judge of the Court of Appeals and the justices of the Appellate Division.

The 470-page report was a sharp indictment of the governor and the state authorities. The commission concluded that the Attica riot was "spontaneous"; it could find no evidence to support Rockefeller's contention that it had been organized and planned by revolutionaries. The riot was "caused by the conditions within the prison."

Other conclusions reached by the McKay Commission were:

The assault itself was not carefully planned to minimize the loss of life: the choice of ammunition and weapons was based upon ready availability, not upon the logic of the specific situation; no safeguards were established to protect against excessive use of force by those who were authorized to fire; no effective control was imposed to prevent firing by those who were not supposed to participate; no adequate arrangements were made for medical care of the severe casualties that should have been anticipated; and no responsible system was established to prevent vengeful reprisals against the inmates after the retaking.

About the actual assault that killed thirty-nine inmates, the commission said:

The deficiencies in the assault plan took their toll in death and injury. The faith of the assault planners in the discretion and restraint of individual troopers proved in many cases to be misplaced. . . . The conclusion is inescapable that there was much unnecessary shooting. Troopers shot into tents, trenches, and barricades without looking first. . . . The use of shotguns loaded with buckshot in the heavily populated spaces of D Yard led to the killing and wounding of hostages and of inmates who were not engaged in any hostile activity. . . .

A final word must be added concerning the exaggerated accounts which troopers gave after the assault to justify the discharge of weapons. Those who fired were never made to feel that absolute candor about what happened was expected of them and, in some cases, a lack of candor was encouraged.

Despite these findings by an independent commission, the all-white grand jury in Wyoming County returned sixty-one indictments. Everyone indicted was an inmate. No state troopers or correction officers were indicted.

COURTS

"In Brooklyn, it's better to know the
judge than to know the law."

—Brooklyn trial lawyer

The Ten
Worst Judges
in New York

THE COURTS are probably the least scrutinized and
the worst functioning institution in New York City. Like
other municipal bureaucracies that process only the powerless—the jails and the municipal hospitals—the courts lack
the white, middle-class victims who generate reform.

To spend a month sitting in the city's courtrooms is to
experience a ninth circle of hell only a Solzhenitsyn or
a Kafka could adequately describe. Routinely, lives are
ruined and families broken by thirty-second decisions. Some
judges quit work at 2:00 P.M. to play golf, while some 8,000
men and women presumed innocent under the Constitution
wait months for trials in the city's overcrowded detention
jails. Other judges have tantrums on the bench and call
defendants "animals" and "scum." Cops pay court attendants ("bridgemen") $5 to call their cases first. Legal Aid
lawyers defend fifty poor clients a day with not a second
for preparation. The bail system lets bondsmen buy freedom
for the rich and the well connected. Clerks sell advance

word on court assignments and decisions. Civil cases almost always get decided in favor of the landlord or businessman or city agency.

The majesty of the Bill of Rights seems remote when you sit in the crowded, noisy Manhattan Criminal Court on Centre Street and watch Legal Aid lawyers walk up and down the aisles calling the names of defendants they have never met but are expected to represent. Meanwhile, cops who should be on the street hang around all day, often dozing, waiting for their arrests to come up on the endless calendar. Finally there is a hurried, whispered negotiation at the bench, and the disposition of the case is agreed on, like some price at an open-air fish market. And then the judge closes the court at 3:00 or 3:30 P.M.

Justice in New York is rarely evenhanded. A black kid from Bed-Stuy gets sentenced to Attica for possession of drugs; the son of a prominent politician gets into a narcotics treatment program and is paroled. In the Bronx, Paul Fino sentences a sick, twenty-three-year-old street junkie to thirty years in prison for the sale of 1/73 of an ounce of heroin. In Brooklyn, Dominic Rinaldi releases a major heroin dealer, with twelve previous arrests, on his own recognizance and without bail. Clifford Irving and his wife are permitted to arrange their jail terms so that one of them will be free to take care of their children. When a lawyer asks a Manhattan Criminal Court judge to do the same thing for a black couple, the plea is rejected.

Scarcely a day now passes without fresh evidence of serious discontent with the courts, not only on the part of victims, but on the part of people in authority. Police Commissioner Patrick Murphy has said: "The courts must accept a giant share of the blame for the continual rise in crime. . . . The whole judicial system is unjust, inefficient and in bankruptcy." Both the Knapp Commission report and the State Commission of Investigation's annual report charged widespread corruption throughout the entire criminal justice system, including the courts. State Senator John Hughes, chairman of the Joint Legislative Committee on Crime, has held hearings on the Mafia's influence on the courts and on judges who have been soft on sentencing heroin dealers. Statistics compiled by the Hughes Committee show that the rate of dismissals and acquittals for Mafiosi in New York City courts is five times higher than the rate for other defendants. During the ten-year period of the study, 1960 through 1969, 44.7 percent of the indictments against organized crime figures were dismissed by local Supreme Court justices. In contrast, only 11.5 percent of the indictments against all defendants were dismissed, according to the committee. For this reason, it is common belief on the streets of this city that judgeships are bought and sold by politicians for cash, and that once on the bench, some judges continue to be up for sale—or at least for rent.

But nothing seems to change because the criticisms are usually general and few individual judges ever get named. Judges are still largely immune to personal attack because of an excessive mystique of respect compounded of tradition and law. We address them as "Your Honor," and we stand deferentially whenever they enter or leave a courtroom. A canon in the legal profession's code of ethics specifically enjoins lawyers from publicly criticizing judges.

All but unknown to most laymen, and virtual dictators

in their courtrooms, many judges feel unaccountable for their conduct. Almost all the Supreme Court justices in the city were picked in closed negotiations among the county political leaders. Most of them had both Democratic and Republican endorsement, and thus could not be opposed by the public at the polls. In fact, many Supreme Court justices have all four parties' support.

Deal-making between the two major parties in the matter of judgeships has a long and dishonorable history. But the individual who has elevated that craft to an art is Nelson Rockefeller. He has played a role in arranging for Republican endorsement of some of the least attractive Democrats —men like Dominic Rinaldi, Aaron Koota, Gerald Culkin. Rockefeller's own appointments to the bench have been, on balance, much worse than John Lindsay's or even Robert Wagner's.

Legal qualifications and the capacity for fair judgment seem to have less to do with who becomes a judge in New York than the right connections—especially family connections. Francis X. Smith is regarded as one of the least qualified Supreme Court justices in Queens; he got his judgeship because his father, Frank V. Smith, was Queens county leader. Guy Mangano is generally considered an inferior Supreme Court justice in Brooklyn; he got his judgeship because of the immense power of his father, James Mangano, who is general clerk of Brooklyn Supreme Court and has been a district leader since 1934. Frank Rossetti, Jr., son of the current leader of Tammany Hall, was appointed to the Court of Claims by Governor Rockefeller as soon as he satisfied the minimum legal requirements for the bench (ten years of practice after being admitted to the bar). Thomas Dickens is a lazy Manhattan Supreme Court justice whose decisions show a high rate of reversals when they are appealed. He is on the bench because his brother was a Harlem district leader and assemblyman. Oliver Sutton is considered a less than adequate Supreme Court justice; his brother Percy, Manhattan borough president, helped secure his judgeship.

Judgeships, in short, have become almost like union cards in the construction trades—private inheritances kept inside the family. And that is one reason why justice continues to be dispensed like remnants from pushcarts.

Of approximately 350 judges working in state and municipal courts in New York City, many are wise in the law, honest, hard-working, free of racism and political influence. There is no discernible pattern, alas, to where these superior judges come from. A few of the best are products of old-line political machines: Irwin Brownstein of the Brooklyn Supreme Court is one; he will always try to place a kid in a narcotics treatment program rather than simply ship him off to jail. Manhattan Supreme Court Justice James Leff is in his chambers at 7:30 every morning. His understanding of the law is evident in brilliant, widely admired decisions. Yet, Leff was attorney for the Conservative party and Carmine De Sapio. Other former regular pols who became superb judges are Vincent Damiani, Mike Castaldi, and Milton Mollen.

On the Civil Court, reform Democrats Irving Younger, Leonard Sandler, and Martin Stecher have been model judges. Republicans Nat Hentel and William Booth are both fine jurists. On the Criminal Court, Lindsay appointees Ernst Rosenberger and Pete McQuillan have raised standards by their presence. And on the Manhattan-Bronx Supreme Court, reformers Samuel Silverman, Arnold Fein, and Edward Greenfield have been outstanding. Former Bronx regular politician David Ross has been superb as the administrator of the Criminal Courts. Ross works eight- and nine-hour days, and his personal assignments are judicious —he buries the bad judges where they can do the least damage.

Who, then, are the worst judges in New York City?

For one straight month, I visited courtrooms, interviewed judges, lawyers, court employees, prosecutors, defendants, and policemen about their experiences in the courts. My purpose was to nominate, by a consensus, the worst of the city's approximately 350 judges.

It was not an easy job. No agency regularly monitors the courts—the press can converge on one sensational trial or another, but it is notoriously indifferent to the trial *system* —and no agency retains records of judicial dispositions. The Bar Association's files of formal complaints against sitting judges are closed to the public. For fear of reprisal, if not out of respect for the code of ethics, no lawyer I spoke to would let himself be quoted by name about a specific judge. And the mystique of respect that allows us to criticize poets, fighters, generals, and presidents, but not judges, silenced some of those who know the inner workings of the courts best.

Nevertheless, enough people, especially several good judges anxious to redeem their own profession, did talk off the record so that a consensus of the worst judges, reinforced by personal observation, finally emerged.

Here, then, are my nominations for the ten worst judges.

Gerald Culkin, Manhattan-Bronx Supreme Court. Culkin, sixty-six years old, is known as the "Watermelon Judge." At a hearing for the Harlem Four in 1968, William Kunstler was seeking Culkin's permission for himself and another lawyer to be assigned as counsel to two of the four defendants. At one point in the proceedings, Culkin turned in his chair and said, to no one in particular, "Those boys wouldn't know a good lawyer from a good watermelon."

Culkin was one of four justices cited by police detectives at a public hearing of Senator John Hughes's Crime Committee in June, 1972, as giving inexplicably lenient sentences to heroin dealers in felony cases. (The next day the *Times* covered the story but did not print Culkin's name.) Culkin is lazy, rarely opening his court before 11:30 A.M. and often sitting less than three hours a day. "The less he works, the better it is for society," says one of his colleagues. Culkin is one of two Supreme Court justices in Manhattan who employ a law secretary who is not a lawyer; he is one Joseph Mariconda.

Over the years Culkin has displayed an extraordinary charity toward members of organized crime. In 1962 he dismissed gambling charges against Joseph Gentile, listed by police as a member of the Mafia family then headed by Joseph Profaci. In 1966 Justice Culkin granted a writ of habeas corpus filed for David Betillo, an associate of Lucky Luciano. In 1968 Justice Culkin ordered a hearing on a writ of error in behalf of mobster Sam Kass, who was serving a term for selling narcotics. All three of these rulings were later reversed by higher courts.

Dan Hoffman, Manhattan Criminal Court. Hoffman was a city marshal for some twenty years before he moved to the bench. He has a law degree but virtually no legal experience as a lawyer. He never had one client or prepared a single memorandum of law. He was very active politically, however. He was appointed by Mayor Lindsay on the recommendation of Republican County Leader Vince Albano. There are those who insist that Hoffman may be the single worst judge in the history of the Manhattan Criminal Court, in terms of his knowledge and understanding of the law.

Wilfred Waltemade, Manhattan-Bronx Supreme Court. With Waltemade presiding over the Matrimonial Part at 60 Centre Street, it's like visiting an insane asylum. Waltemade screams at the top of his lungs at defendants, lawyers, even court clerks and stenographers. Anything can set off one of his tantrums. He seems totally irrational, the most visibly unstable Supreme Court justice in the city. He destroys the dignity of the law. He habitually addresses black defendants by their first names and calls white defendants "Mister."

Waltemade is also lazy. One day I observed him open his court at 11:30 A.M., take lunch from 12:45 to 2:15 P.M., and then quit at 3:15 P.M. Another day he kept the same schedule, except that he stopped at 3:55 P.M. (Article One of the General Rules of the Judicial Conference says that daily sessions of the courts shall not be less than six hours.)

Waltemade got his judgeship through the wisdom of the late Bronx boss Charles Buckley.

Dominic Rinaldi, Brooklyn Supreme Court. Rinaldi is very tough on long-haired attorneys and black defendants, especially on questions of bail, probation, and sentencing. But his judicial temper softens remarkably before heroin dealers and organized crime figures.

In August of 1972, Rinaldi released Norman Burton—a junk dealer with twelve previous arrests who was up on a charge of possession of heroin and attempted bribery of the cop who arrested him—with no bail.* In October of 1970, Rinaldi let a drug dealer named Clifton Glover plead guilty and then gave him a conditional discharge. Glover had two prior arrests for selling heroin, and he could have been sentenced to twenty-five years. According to John O'Connor, the executive director of the Hughes Committee, "A conditional discharge for a C felony is prohibited under the state's Penal Law." During the summer Rinaldi sits in Suffolk County. In 1967 he caused a local scandal there when he permitted three prominent organized crime figures charged with bribery and conspiracy to plead guilty to misdemeanors and let them go free with only $250 fines. The district attorney thought the three (Paul Vario, James Marinacci, and Benjamin Greenfeder) should have gotten at least one year in jail.

Albert Bosch, Queens Supreme Court. Bosch, like Rinaldi, is very harsh on the average defendant. He is famous for revoking bail or parole at the start of trials, even if the defendant has made all prior court appearances and has roots in the community. But he shows mysterious compas-

---

* Burton has since fled the court's jurisdiction and there is now a warrant out for his arrest.

sion for certain heroin dealers. Bosch was severely criticized by the State Commission of Investigation in its annual report, released August 13, 1972, for his handling of one particular felony case. Bosch permitted a police detective named Joseph DeVito, who had Mafia connections and was charged with conspiracy to sell a half pound of heroin (a felony), to plead guilty to a misdemeanor. Bosch let DeVito off with a suspended sentence, imposing only the condition that DeVito resign from the force. He could have given him four years in prison.

The State Commission's report said of Justice Bosch:

Judge Bosch's claim that he did not know the DeVito case involved heroin is not in accord with the information contained in the indictment, which the Judge had before him at the time of sentencing.

It is also a claim which contradicts the Judge's own remarks, which preceded his pronouncement of sentence, when he stated, "I have examined the background of the defendant. . . ."

Not only was DeVito's misdemeanor plea accepted, but the Judge imposed sentence on the same day, without waiting for the probation report. There would appear to be no justification for the haste which surrounded the unusual events of the day.

Philip Zichello, Manhattan Civil Court. Zichello, sixty-seven, was the deputy commissioner of hospitals in 1950 when he came under investigation by a grand jury for ties with the Mafia. District Attorney Frank Hogan charged that Zichello had met secretly with mobsters Joey Rao and Joe Stretch. Hogan called the meeting "a shocking example of notorious racketeers helping to influence a political decision." Zichello was then fired by Mayor Impellitteri.

In 1969, after the judicial nominating convention had

been held, Zichello was suddenly put up by the Democrats for the Civil Court in Manhattan to fill a vacancy. As a result, Zichello had no opposition on the ballot and couldn't lose. Nevertheless, he was vigorously opposed by the New York Bar Association and *The New York Times*.

In three years on the Civil Court, Zichello has repeatedly shown that he is clearly unfit. In the fall of 1971, a group of antipoverty lawyers backed a formal complaint against him because of his explosive temper and consistent bias in favor of landlords. In that same year, more than half of his decisions in landlord cases that were appealed were reversed by the appellate court.

Zichello got his judgeship as a result of an understanding between Tammany leader Frank Rossetti and Republican County Chairman Vince Albano. Albano apparently made sure Zichello had no opposition in 1969. At the time, Zichello's law partner was a Republican district leader.

George Postel, Manhattan-Bronx Supreme Court. Postel, sixty, presided at the extortion and conspiracy trial of the famous Mafioso Carmine Persico in November of 1971. First, Postel barred the press from the trial, threatening to throw journalists "in the can." Then he undercut the prosecution's case by quashing a subpoena of its best witness against Persico. Persico was acquitted. A month later the Court of Appeals called Postel's eviction of all reporters a violation of the First Amendment.

Like Judge Culkin, Postel has a law secretary who is not even a lawyer. This is apparent in his written decisions, the objects of derisive laughter from lawyers who must read them.

Postel was first appointed as a magistrate by Robert Wagner in 1955. He is up for re-election to the Supreme Court in 1974.

Edward Dudley, Manhattan-Bronx Supreme Court. Dudley has a great reputation—former envoy to Africa, former borough president of Manhattan, former administrative judge for the Criminal Court, current administrative judge for the Manhattan-Bronx Supreme Court. But Dudley is an example of what Jimmy Breslin calls "upward failure." Having proved inept in one slot, he keeps getting promoted to a higher one.

Every Supreme Court justice I talked to was bitter about Dudley's incompetence and his undeservedly high reputation. They blame much of the chaos and backlog in their courts on Dudley's laziness, his inability to make wise judicial assignments, his inability to bolster morale. Says one judge: "Dudley doesn't know who works and who doesn't work because he's never here himself. He plays golf avidly and often. He sits in court only three weeks a year, and that's to give out patronage. And Dudley insisted he be given a limousine and a chauffeur when he first took the job. His predecessor [Saul Streit] didn't have either."

Dudley became administrator of the Supreme Court in the face of a study prepared for Mayor Lindsay by Columbia University in October of 1970; the report called for Dudley's removal as administrator of the Criminal Courts.

Despite the enormous backlog of cases, Dudley spent six weeks during the summer of 1972 on an ocean cruise. "This was the most important six weeks of the year," said one judge. "We were starting the new narcotics parts. It was a new experiment. We needed someone to make the assignments and allocate manpower. And there was Dudley sailing for six weeks. It was a crime."

Paul Fino, Manhattan-Bronx Supreme Court. Fino is a politician. He simply does not know the law. A former congressman and Republican county leader of the Bronx, he virtually appointed himself to the court. Of the thirty lawyers I interviewed for this article, all but two said Fino was among the worst judges in the city. There was more negative unanimity on him than on any other judge. When he was nominated for the Supreme Court in 1968, the Bar Association reported Fino as unqualified for the bench. *The New York Times* also opposed his self-nomination. In January of 1972, Fino's imposition of a thirty-year prison sentence on Jerry Williams, a twenty-three-year-old addict convicted of selling 1/73 of an ounce of heroin—with no evidence the addict was a major dealer—was so outrageous that even the tough Bronx district attorney, Burton Roberts, protested Fino's action. Fino, in turn, absurdly accused Roberts of "pampering criminals."

John Monteleone, Brooklyn Supreme Court. Monteleone's handling of two recent proceedings would seem to be the stuff of which impeachment cases are made.

The first I learned of through an outraged employee of the Probation Department. Al Cohen, according to police records, a racketeer affiliated with the Mafia family of Joe Colombo, pleaded guilty to two burglary counts. Cohen offered to become a police informer, but the police became convinced that he really wanted to become a double agent

—to continue to serve the mob. At the time of the plea, the district attorney's office asked Justice Monteleone to impose the maximum sentence (four years) on Cohen, in part because of Cohen's highly questionable double-agent ploy. Instead, Justice Monteleone gave Cohen a suspended sentence, on the astonishing ground that he had cooperated with the police.

The second questionable case involved Frank Cangiano, an alleged member of the Vito Genovese family charged with criminal possession of forged money instruments. Cangiano had been indicted on April 15, 1970, and for the next eighteen months he kept winning adjournments—at least thirteen—from various judges on the request of his lawyers. In October, 1971, the case came before Justice Monteleone. Brooklyn District Attorney Eugene Gold asked for an adjournment—the first such request from the state. Justice Monteleone immediately threw the case out of court —on grounds of failure to prosecute. To his credit, Gold appealed the decision. The Appellate Division unanimously ruled that the indictment against Cangiano be reinstated. The case is still pending.

Monteleone was elevated from the Civil Court bench to the Supreme Court by Brooklyn County Leader Meade Esposito in 1970. He also had Republican backing.

The failure of the courts hurts the whole city. One reason the jails are ripe for revolt is the sloth of the judges. One reason heroin causes muggings in the streets and teenage ODs in the ghetto is the coddling by judges of the big-time merchants of death. One reason organized crime flourishes is the permissiveness, or corruption, of some judges. One reason citizens don't feel safe on the streets is that the best cops, the ones who make the most arrests, are tied up in court waiting for judges to start work.

Reform of any institution is long, difficult, and costly. But three things can be done quickly to improve our miserable court system. Two of these reforms won't cost the taxpayer a cent.

First, we must end the practice of allowing politicians to pick our judges. Impartial screening committees of lawyers and community leaders should recommend judicial candidates based solely on the standard of legal excellence.

Second, citizens should participate in monitoring the courts. This is the best way to make judges feel accountable —let them know they are being watched by the public. If there are ten blacks sitting in a courtroom, it will be harder for Justice Rinaldi to let a heroin dealer go. If there are ten law students, it will be harder for Justice Culkin to rule favorably on a gangster's writ.

Jack Weinstein, the very able federal judge in the Eastern District, suggests that New York copy the system California uses to monitor performance on the bench. That is, a permanent committee of lawyers and laymen, with a full-time staff, would receive complaints and have the power to discipline or remove judges for cause.

Third, there must be better supervision and administration of the courts. Upward failures like Justice Dudley should be fired. Administrative judges who will keep the courts open twenty-four hours a day, not just four, must be appointed. Round-the-clock courts are obviously one way —admittedly at some cost—to relieve the acute pressure on our overcrowded jails.

CRUEL AND UNUSUAL JUSTICE

As matters now stand, justice in New York is not only blind, it is too often deaf, dumb, and bought.

October 16, 1972

POSTSCRIPT

Independent evidence of the sloth of judges was published on the front page of *The New York Times* on June 6, 1973. A story by David Burnham based on a management study conducted by the prestigious Economic Development Council showed that in the Manhattan Supreme Court, judges spend an average of three hours and twenty-one minutes a day on the bench. (Again, the General Rules of the Judicial Conference state that daily court sessions shall total not less than six hours.) The study, conducted in December of 1972, was leaked to the press after the presiding justices refused to release it.

Among the major reasons for the low productivity, according to the study, was that so many judges came to work late. The report concluded, "We believe that the court utilization study reaffirms the critical need for improved organization and management within the courts."

But the fact that court administrators covered up this harsh report rather than acting on its sound recommendations suggests that court reform—even at the management level—is doubtful under the existing judicial establishment.

Two months after the publication of this piece, Paul Fino resigned from the Supreme Court. In June of 1973, he ran in the Republican primary in the Bronx for councilman-at-large. Fino was defeated by a political unknown, Pasquale Mele.

The same week he lost to Mele, Fino's decision in the Jerry Williams case was reversed by a five-member appeals court. The thirty-year sentence Fino had imposed was reduced to an indeterminate term of no more than seven years. In overturning Fino's verdict, the appeals court criticized Fino for forbidding Williams's defense attorney from questioning prospective jurors about whether they were prejudiced against blacks.

On November 1, 1973, the Joint Legislative Committee on Crime conducted a public hearing. At that hearing, facts were revealed that showed Queens Supreme Court Justice Albert Bosch released eight Mafia members on probation and a fine of $2,500 each after they had pled guilty to hijacking $100,000 worth of clothing.

While on probation, the eight mobsters were arrested eighteen times for such crimes as auto theft, bribery, burglary, and more hijacking. Despite these crimes, they remained free on probation. They remained on probation at the discretion of Justice Bosch.

The only reaction to these disclosures was an editorial in the *Daily News*. The Queens Bar Association and Presiding Justice Samuel Rabin remained conspicuously silent.

Justice
Gets a Fix

NORMAN BURTON is a heroin dealer in the asphalt colony called Bedford-Stuyvesant. On a good day he will sell $4,000 worth of junk out of the brownstone he owns at 553A Monroe Street.

On August 8, 1972, Burton was in court. It was his 13th arrest. His five-page yellow sheet showed convictions for selling heroin, for check forgery, and for assault. On this occasion he was charged with selling heroin and bribing a policeman; he had offered the arresting officer $1,000, and it was recorded on tape.

But Norman Burton was released without bail. He may now be back on the mean streets of Bed-Stuy selling junk to twelve-year-olds. The judge who let Burton go without any bail was Dominic Rinaldi, a justice in Brooklyn Supreme Court.

This was not the first time Judge Rinaldi has let a heroin dealer go free. He has a reputation among lawyers and court reformers for going soft on pushers, especially when they are represented by certain well-connected bail bondsmen and lawyers.

On June 15, 1972, at a public hearing of the Joint Legislative Committee on Crime, Rinaldi was one of four city judges named publicly as being suspiciously lenient in felony narcotics cases.

Dominic Rinaldi is a loyal part of the Brooklyn political machine. He is especially close to County Leader Meade Esposito and to James Mangano. Mangano, a district leader and the chief clerk of Brooklyn Supreme Court, has been a great conservative power in borough politics for twenty years; his son Guy Mangano is also a Brooklyn Supreme Court judge.

Despite Rinaldi's kindness to big heroin dealers, he has displayed little compassion when it comes to youthful offenders, bail for poor people, or inmate rights. He has also been more anxious to sentence young drug addicts to the dungeon of Rikers Island than to put them in narcotics treatment programs.

Says a wise political lawyer, "Compared with the good Supreme Court judges in Brooklyn, compared with Thomas Jones, or Irwin Brownstein, or Abe Kalina, Rinaldi is totally insensitive to civil liberties."

Two weeks after Rinaldi released Burton without bail, Billy David was asked about the Burton case in Red-Stuy's old, run-down 79th Precinct at the corner of Gates and Throop. David is a black plainclothes anticrime cop specializing in narcotics. He made the Burton arrest.

"We were trying to get Norman for a month. I had arrested him once before, as he was selling a $5 bag to a twelve-year-old boy. Once we staked out his house and watched seventy-five people buy drugs from him in two hours. I watched college girls drive up in VWs and buy heroin from him. Anyway, the first time we arrested him, he was given only $1,500 bail, and he had that much in cash on him.

"It was hard to bust Norman because he almost never leaves his house, and we knew he carried a gun. We finally got him as he was bringing back twenty-five decks of heroin from his supplier. . . .

"A few days later, I received word that Norman wanted to see me and make a deal. I reported this to the Police Department's Internal Affairs Division, and they had me wear a wire [concealed tape recorder] when I met with Norman.

"When I saw him, Norman offered me $1,000 to drop the case by not showing up in court. At that point I arrested him for bribery."

Norman Burton's arraignment was on August 8, 1972, in Brooklyn. Billy David decided to go to the hearing because he was curious how Norman managed to get such low bail the last time.

In the middle of the hearing, Judge Rinaldi was told by Norman's lawyer that David was in the courtroom, and Rinaldi ordered David to the bench.

"The judge started to yell at me," David recalls. "He asked me what was I doing there, and then he asked me three times what bail should be set for Norman. I felt humiliated. I felt that I was nothing. The judge was yelling at me, and Norman was watching, and other defendants were watching. I couldn't even talk I felt so bad. Then Judge Rinaldi let Norman off with no bail. He paroled him in his own custody. I will never forget the tone of contempt in Rinaldi's voice as he was yelling at me. The other guy was selling heroin to children and I was being treated as the criminal."

David's commanding officer, Sergeant Tom Santise, was outraged when he learned what happened in court. He filed an immediate complaint with Inspector Eli Lazarus of the Criminal Justice Bureau. He also called the Brooklyn DA's office to express his dismay. The DA's office reassured Santise there was nothing improper about David's presence in the courtroom at the arraignment.

The Joint Legislative Committee on Crime, chaired by Republican State Senator John Hughes of Syracuse, has been investigating felony narcotics cases (a felony is possession of more than a pound of hard drugs) in which dealers have escaped jail sentences. The committee has a file on Judge Rinaldi.

Clifton Glover is a heroin dealer on about the same scale of operation as Norman Burton—considerably above the typical street-corner addict-pusher. Glover was arrested in Brooklyn on May 20, 1970, for selling narcotics. An undercover cop made a buy and then arrested Glover. Glover had on him two ounces of heroin, almost a pound of cocaine, and a loaded gun. He had two prior arrests for selling drugs and was free on bail at the time of his arrest. Glover himself was not an addict.

On October 28, 1970, Glover appeared before Judge Rinaldi. He pleaded guilty and received a conditional discharge—no sentence. He could have received up to twenty-five years. According to John O'Connor, the executive director of the Joint Committee on Crime, "A conditional discharge for a C felony is prohibited under the state's penal law."

In December, 1971, the Joint Committee released a study of court dispositions of felony narcotics cases. The study revealed that in Brooklyn only 6 percent of major narcotics dealers are sentenced to a year or more in prison. This compares with 31 percent in the Bronx and 28 percent in Queens. The same survey disclosed that 42 percent of felony narcotics cases in Brooklyn were dismissed, compared with only 15 percent in the Bronx.

Two related poisons are eating away at New York—the plague of heroin and the corruption of the criminal justice system caused by the billion-dollar economy of junk. After reading the Joint Crime Committee's studies, and the State Commission of Investigation's annual report released in August, 1972, it seems clear that the most dangerous corrupters of justice in this town are not the cops on the beat, but those who are more powerful and respectable—the judges and prosecutors.*

Heroin kills. It causes crime, it destroys neighborhoods, it makes citizens flee to the suburbs or live in fear behind triple locks. One child a week dies in this city because of the negligence of drug-addicted parents. Of the inmates in the overcrowded Tombs, 80 percent are junkies. More than half of the fifty-eight homicides during one recent week involved heroin. The economy of junk is what organized

---

* The State Commission's report devoted thirty-two pages to describing how the Queens district attorney's office and Judge Albert Bosch let a heroin dealer plead guilty to a misdemeanor and go free.

crime is all about. And the immense profits of heroin corrupt the rule of law itself.

There are at least 250,000 heroin addicts in New York City. Nobody knows for sure, just as nobody knows for sure exactly how many rats are in the slums. It is estimated by Max Singer of the Hudson Institute that in New York State, addicts steal a half billion dollars annually to maintain their habits.

So what Judge Rinaldi is doing is no small thing. He is putting people on the street who sell death for a profit. (Glover, remember, was not an addict but a businessman.) Just look at Fox Street in the South Bronx, or Myrtle Avenue in Bed-Stuy, and you can see the process of generational genocide caused by heroin. Ten-year-olds dead of ODs in abandoned buildings and alleys. Storekeepers murdered by addicts desperate for a fix. Old junkies dead at thirty with no veins left.

Thanks to David Durk, Frank Serpico, David Burnham, and the Knapp Commission, police corruption has been exposed to public scrutiny. Norman Burton was not merely a heroin dealer. He tried to bribe a cop, and the cop reported it and took some risk to make an additional arrest for bribery. What Billy David did was exemplary. But Judge Rinaldi abused him and let the briber go free. What effect will the example set by Judge Rinaldi have on cynical cops tempted by graft?

Billy David is not affluent. Norman Burton, the dealer, probably makes $100,000 a year; he owns two houses. Billy David should have been honored for arresting Norman Burton. Instead, Judge Rinaldi made him feel like a criminal.

Billy David and other good cops are society's garbagemen. They do the shit work and take risks no one else wants. They aren't responsible for the poverty and violence of Bedford-Stuyvesant; they didn't build the rotten housing, or cause the unemployment, or bring in all the narcotics and knives, or spread the venereal diseases, or breed the rats. The banks and the real estate speculators and the politicians did that. Billy David just goes out every night and tries to protect people from muggers and robbers, and tries to lock up the heroin dealers.

Unlike most of us, he gets to see the victims—the mother whose son is strung out on junk, the old person killed for $2, a welfare recipient whose check has been stolen, the ODs still in public school. And in the 79th Precinct all the victims are black.

Nobody judges the judges. A Supreme Court justice like Dominic Rinaldi is literally beyond the law. He is a king without accountability. As long as he pleases Meade Esposito and James Mangano, he will remain a judge. And you and I will have to stand in respect every time he enters and leaves his courtroom.

August 31, 1972

POSTSCRIPT

During the fall of 1972, I wrote three more articles detailing suspiciously lenient decisions by Justice Rinaldi. Two of these cases involved Mafia members Paul Vario and Sal Agro, and a third involved a narcotics dealer named Clifton Glover.

On November 12, 1973, Judge Rinaldi was indicted on

three counts of perjury by a grand jury impaneled by Special State Prosecutor Maurice Nadjari. He was also indicted on one count of obstruction of justice. The perjury involved criminal cases Judge Rinaldi was suspected of fixing. If convicted on all counts, Judge Rinaldi can be sentenced to twenty-two years in prison.

My series on Justice Rinaldi began by accident. I had spent many hot nights during the summer of 1972 riding around the 79th Precinct in Bed-Stuy with an anticrime police sergeant named Tom Santise. Santise was a good cop, and I wanted to write a piece about him. He was honest and brave, and he had an impossible job.

One night he mentioned casually that one of the plainclothes narcotics cops who worked under him had had a painful experience in court that morning. The cop, named Billy David, had arrested a heroin dealer for possession of drugs and for bribery. But the judge had let the dealer walk free without any bail, and then abused and insulted the cop for being present in the courtroom at the time of arraignment.

The judge who did that was Dominic Rinaldi. I spent the next several weeks carefully analyzing records of Judge Rinaldi's previous dispositions.

Gradually, a disturbing pattern emerged. Blacks and Puerto Ricans got high bail and long sentences. Defendants connected with organized crime families were treated permissively—motions granted, misdemeanor pleas accepted, suspended sentences given, fines imposed instead of jail terms. Occasionally large-scale heroin dealers would get inexplicably lenient sentences, even conditional discharges, for Class A narcotics felonies. And certain Brooklyn lawyers would almost always win their cases before Rinaldi.

My instincts smelled a rat. I decided to begin a personal crusade to alert the judicial, legal, and political establishments to this incompetent and probably corrupt member of the judiciary. I wrote four articles in the *Voice* and one in *New York* magazine detailing cases in which Judge Rinaldi had acted suspiciously and in ways that defied law and reason.

I have a theory of muckraking that says writing an article of exposure is less than half the job—creating a constituency for an idea by lobbying and writing repeated follow-up articles is crucial. The journalist, if serious, should also be an activist; that is the only way actually to affect events and institutions. Any personality, or any bureaucracy, can easily survive one critical article.

So as part of my effort against Judge Rinaldi I went on several television shows, including an excellent documentary by Jeff Kamen on WNET, and on radio WBAI to spread information about the judge's indiscretions. I also spoke at several forums of lawyers, including the Brandeis Association and Brooklyn Law School, expanding on my original articles with new research.

The *Voice* also generously took out full-page ads in *The New York Times Book Review* and in the *New York Review of Books,* focusing still greater attention on the doubtful quality of justice in Rinaldi's courtroom.

Nevertheless, the appropriate establishments did not respond. They seemed bereft of curiosity. If I had published such serious allegations of misconduct against a cop, or a sanitation worker, I'm sure some authority would have asked me to produce the evidence.

But a judge comes from a more elite social and economic class.

I had the naive expectation that Sam Rabin, the presiding justice for the Second Department, might call me. The articles had stirred up considerable public interest. (I had personally received more than seventy-five letters.) Perhaps Rabin might be curious about the specifics of the cases I wrote about. He was, technically, Rinaldi's boss.

When Rabin did not call me, I called him. Once, twice, three times, a fourth time. He would never call back. I could get Mayor Lindsay, or Ted Kennedy, even Ralph Nader on the phone. But Sam Rabin was "busy" for three weeks. I wanted to show the evidence, the official court transcripts, to Rabin. I wanted him to see how Rinaldi ignored recommendations from the district attorney and the Probation Department. Rabin had the power to remove or investigate Rinaldi. He was one of the most respected and powerful jurists in the state. But I could not get him on the phone.

Justice Rabin knew, on a social basis, some people I also knew. I sent messages through them to him, asking him to please return my calls. He told these mutual acquaintances I was wrong, and irresponsible, and he would not dignify my yellow journalism with an interview.

I asked a judge, a friend of Rabin's, to talk to him. The judge reported back that Rabin would only talk to me if I was planning to write something critical about him personally.

One last time I called the chambers of Presiding Justice Rabin. I spoke to his assistant, Sheldon Amster. I said that any time in the next month, at the judge's convenience, I would go anywhere to interview him about why he hadn't investigated the specific cases involving Justice Rinaldi I had written about. I was never called back.

The Brooklyn Bar Association also had some responsibility: they could investigate or censure Justice Rinaldi. But instead, the Brooklyn Bar approved and distributed a report attacking my articles as "malicious, unfounded, and irresponsible."

The report for the Brooklyn Bar was written by Howard Kass, a "Court Street" lawyer with ties to the Brooklyn clubhouses. Kass wrote his report without interviewing me or any of the cops involved in the four cases I wrote about. He did not interview Brooklyn District Attorney Eugene Gold. He did not interview anyone on the staff of Special Prosecutor Maurice Nadjari. In fact, the only person Howard Kass interviewed was Judge Dominic Rinaldi.

The report, dated November 13, 1972, concluded: "False and misleading articles must be stopped by the Association of the Bar, if we, the lawyers and judges, are to command and retain the respect, confidence, and trust of the public. Articles such as these demand condemnation by the Bar Association."

I was not sent a copy of the report. I heard about it and asked Kass's office to send me a copy so that I might reply. I was told the report clearing Rinaldi was "confidential."

After my third article on Judge Rinaldi appeared, I received a message that Brooklyn County Leader Meade

Esposito wanted to "straighten me out" about the Brooklyn judiciary.

So I met Esposito for lunch on Montague Street in Brooklyn. Esposito, a charming con artist, started by telling me about all the "great judges we got in Brooklyn." He added that he personally hadn't set foot in the courthouse in five years.

I then asked him about Rinaldi.

"I hardly know the guy," Meade said. "He got made before I became the leader."

That was not true. Esposito and Rinaldi were intimate friends. They had summer houses a few miles apart and spent many weekends sailing together. Esposito had used his considerable influence in 1966 to get Rinaldi appointed to a prestigious state commission on court reform.

I also knew that Esposito had been questioned in executive session by the Joint Legislative Committee on Crime about his possible role in trying to fix one of the cases involving Justice Rinaldi that I had written about (the Sal Agro case, in which Agro, a Mafioso indicted for grand larceny and forgery, pled guilty and was given a suspended sentence by Rinaldi).

Esposito, on that occasion, had admitted he was friends with Rinaldi, and he admitted that Agro's lawyer, Stanley Reiben, had met with him the night before Agro was given a suspended sentence by Rinaldi.

I told Meade I did not believe Rinaldi was a stranger to him.

"Well, off the record, Jack, I do know the guy pretty good. But listen to me, please lay off him. The guy has got a retarded son, and he has terrible grief. Be a nice guy,

Jack, and don't write no more about Rinaldi. As a favor. He got a retarded kid."

Justice Rinaldi does have a son with a mental problem. The son has a patronage job in the Brooklyn Supreme Court.

By the start of 1973, I felt at a dead end in my obsession to expose Judge Rinaldi. I felt as if I had been throwing snowballs at dinosaurs.

My research had convinced me that Rinaldi was as bad as a judge could be. But as a sitting judge, with powerful political connections, Rinaldi seemed—and acted—beyond accountability.

The institutions of possible remedy—the presiding justice, the Brooklyn Bar, and the Brooklyn Democratic machine—all seemed anxious to cover up for Rinaldi. The state legislature has the power to impeach a judge, but the only lawmaker who ever talked to me about the Rinaldi articles was Manhattan Assemblyman Tony Olivieri.

Al Blumenthal, Jerry Kretchmer, and Robert Postel, then running for the mayoral nomination, all criticized Rinaldi in speeches. The suddenly aggressive Appellate Division wrote each of them letters demanding proof or an apology —and then leaked the letters to the *Daily News*. Kretchmer wrote a long letter back, citing cases and quoting transcripts. He received no answer. He wrote another letter asking for an investigation. Still no response from the superjudges who run the court system.

By April of 1973, I had given up hope; then I learned that Special Prosecutor Nadjari was beginning a grand jury investigation into Justice Rinaldi.

In May of 1973 Judge Rinaldi filed a $6 million lawsuit against *The Village Voice* for defamation and invasion of privacy.

Over the next six months there were lengthy discovery hearings in which Rinaldi and I were examined under oath by lawyers. During these hearings, Rinaldi admitted the essential facts of the four articles I wrote about him were true.

Rinaldi admitted that the conditional discharge he gave a heroin dealer named Clifton Glover for a Class A felony was illegal. Glover, a big-time narcotics wholesaler, was not an addict himself. Rinaldi also admitted he gave no jail sentence to Mafioso Paul Vario, even though the district attorney had requested a jail sentence. (Vario had a prior conviction for rape.) And Rinaldi admitted he gave mobster Sal Agro a suspended sentence despite the fact that the written probation report recommended a jail term for Agro, who had a long criminal record.

After one of these pretrial examinations, Rinaldi said to me: "You're persecuting me. I didn't do nothing wrong. I'm an honest man. I'm going to be renominated next year, and I'm going to be re-elected, and that will vindicate me. [Rinaldi's fourteen-year term expires in 1974.] You and that Village rag are full of hot air."

He did not say he expected to win his lawsuit.

A few weeks later a Brooklyn politician told me: "Meade [Esposito] says he's going to put Rinaldi back on the bench. He says you're persecuting Rinaldi. And he's really pissed at you. He called you a 'demented, fuckin' Trotsky.' "

I assumed by "Trotsky" Meade really meant Jew Communist.

More recently Esposito has been calling the bearded Sam Roberts of the *Daily News* "Rasputin."

If I'm Trotsky, and Roberts is Rasputin, that makes Meade Esposito the Tsar.

And we all know what happened to the Tsar.

Brooklyn is, and has been for years, the most corrupt county in New York City, rivaling Chicago, Albany, Maryland, and New Jersey in venality.

There are certain historic reasons for this. Brooklyn is the some base for three Mafia families—the Gambinos, the Colombos, and the Gallos. The modern Brooklyn Democratic party has never been cleansed by a period of reform. And the Brooklyn machine is strengthened by an infrastructure of business institutions: Local 1814 of the ILA; the American Bank and Trust Company and the Kings Lafayette Bank; and the Grand Agency, an insurance company owned jointly by Assemblyman Stanley Steingut and County Leader Esposito.

Moreover, the Brooklyn Bar Association acts as if the Canons of Judicial Ethics and the Constitution don't apply to the Brooklyn judiciary. And the Police Department in Brooklyn has a long history of graft, from Boss Tweed to the Knapp Commission hearings.

The 1973 accounting of public corruption indictments in Brooklyn is staggering. Two congressmen, two judges, two city marshals, one city commissioner, one assemblyman, and nineteen policemen. Many of the indictments linked the miscreants to the Mafia.

The way things are going, next year's annual dinner of the Kings County Democracy may be held in Attica.

Judge Corso
and the Mafia

D URING the last eighteen months, five criminal indictments against Mafia members in Brooklyn have been thrown out of court by the trial judge. All five were later unanimously reinstated by the Appellate Division. And all five dismissals were ordered by the same Brooklyn Supreme Court justice—Joseph Corso.

Joseph Caruso, an alleged soldier in the Carlo Gambino Mafia family, was indicted for contempt in Brooklyn. On March 1, 1971, Caruso pleaded guilty before Judge Corso. On September 29, 1971, in a highly unusual procedure, Judge Corso permitted Caruso to change his mind and withdraw his plea, and then dismissed the indictment against him. On June 12, 1972, the Appellate Division reversed Corso's decision in a 5–0 ruling. Then, on September 15, 1972, Judge Corso let Caruso plead guilty again and fined him $500. According to a witness in court that day, "By the time Corso said the word 'five,' Caruso had the money, five new $100 bills, out of his pocket, and handed it over."

Vincent De Cicco, listed by police as a button man for

the Gambino family, was convicted of contempt of a Brooklyn grand jury on September 24, 1971. Judge Corso threw out the jury's verdict and dismissed the indictment. To his considerable credit, Brooklyn District Attorney Eugene Gold appealed Corso's ruling, as he appealed all five of these curious Corso dismissals. And the Appellate Division unanimously reversed Judge Corso, restoring the guilty decision and reinstating the original indictment.

On June 1, 1972, De Cicco came before Judge Corso for sentencing. Prior to the sentencing date, Gold sent Judge Corso a written recommendation from the Probation Department that the defendant be sentenced to the maximum, a year in jail, based partly on the fact that De Cicco's criminal record began in 1931 and included a conviction for robbery. Judge Corso instead imposed a three-month sentence.

In this case Judge Corso admits he spoke to the Probation Department, but he says he was given a recommendation for a more lenient sentence. Judge Corso has refused, however, to say with whom he spoke in the Probation Department. And a Probation Department employee told me: "I don't believe anyone here would have recommended lenience for a guy like De Cicco. We believe Judge Corso can probably cite some legal justification for his decision, but I will always be suspicious of him because of his special zeal in this case. He went out of his way to help De Cicco."

Bruno Capio is listed as a soldier in the Bonanno family. His contempt indictment was dismissed by Judge Corso on November 9, 1971, and was reinstated on the district attorney's appeal on April 10, 1972. The case is still pending in the Brooklyn courts.

Aniello Dellacroce is one of the major figures in organized crime; he is regarded as the underboss of the whole Carlo Gambino family. His contempt indictment was thrown out by Judge Corso on February 2, 1971, and then unanimously reinstated by the Appellate Division on February 7, 1972.

Angelo Sparaco is listed by law enforcement agencies as a *capo* in the Bonanno family. Judge Corso dismissed his indictment on June 7, 1971, and the Appellate Division unanimously reinstated the indictment on May 15, 1972. The case is still pending.

Judge Corso's extraordinary permissiveness toward the Mafia is inconsistent with his treatment of other defendants. And inconsistent with his record while he was an assemblyman.

Dan Alterman, an attorney affiliated with the Lawyers Guild, tells this story of his experience before Judge Corso: "I had a client, a black kid, nineteen years old. He was in the hospital, on the critical list, as the result of a fight on the street. While he was in the hospital, he obviously was unable to report to his probation officer. We appeared before Judge Corso on a violation of probation charge. Judge Corso wouldn't even listen to us. He told my client, 'You deserve to be put away,' and sent my client back to prison."

Corso's record as an assemblyman was undistinguished, except for one bill he would introduce every session of the legislature. The Corso bill would permit public school teachers to hit students, to use "reasonable force."

In 1957 the bill was vetoed by Governor Harriman, and in 1959 and again in 1960 Corso's corporal punishment bill was killed by Governor Rockefeller, after the New York Board of Education and the *Herald Tribune* urged its veto.

The Joint Legislative Committee on Crime, chaired by Republican John Hughes of Syracuse, has been compiling statistics on the quality of justice in the courts. The facts suggest there is something rotten in the judiciary, particularly in Brooklyn.

According to the Hughes Committee's records, Mafia members and big-time heroin dealers are systematically treated more leniently than other defendants. In New York City, 44.7 percent of indictments against organized crime figures during the last ten years were dismissed by State Supreme Court justices. In contrast, only 11.5 percent of the indictments against all defendants were dismissed. In 193 cases where Mafiosi were actually convicted by a jury, the study showed that the trial judge let the defendants off with no prison sentence 46 percent of the time. Another study prepared by the Hughes Committee staff showed that major heroin dealers are treated more permissively by judges in Brooklyn than in any other county in the city.

Only 6 percent of the heroin dealers charged with a felony received more than one year in prison from Brooklyn judges. In contrast, 31.6 percent of the felony heroin defendants in the Bronx were sentenced to more than a year in prison. Brooklyn judges dismissed 42 percent of the felony cases against heroin dealers, while only 15 percent of such cases were thrown out by Bronx judges.

The point is not that all judges should become tougher on all defendants. In selected areas—like heroin traffic and organized crime—judges should be less permissive. But at the same time, in other areas—sentencing first offenders, considering alternatives to detention, setting bail for poor people, handling addicts who are not large-scale pushers—in these areas, judges should be more flexible and more compassionate. The problem now is that some judges have completely reversed the areas where toughness and sensitivity are required, so that the law has a double standard—one for the underboss of the Carlo Gambino family, another for a black kid from Bed-Stuy on probation.

A federal prosecutor, one of several law enforcement officials currently investigating the criminal justice system in New York City, had this to say:

"Brooklyn is the worst, a special case for several reasons. One, the mob has always had deep roots in Brooklyn—the Gallos, Colombos, and the Gambino family particularly. Second, as the Knapp hearings showed, there is a long history of police corruption in Brooklyn. Third, the Brooklyn Bar Association is really venal and has never helped in keeping the courts clean. And fourth, there is no tradition in Brooklyn of keeping politics out of the courts. The machine gets most of its patronage from the courts. Personally, as a prosecutor, I will not take an organized crime case into Brooklyn Supreme Court. There are too many contract judges there. Carlo Gambino can probably influence more judges there than the DA's office."

In fairness, it should be pointed out there are also some excellent Supreme Court judges in Brooklyn. Irwin Brownstein is remarkable for his knowledge of the law and his commitment to equal justice. Milton Mollen, Vincent Damiani, and Tom Jones are also highly qualified Brooklyn Supreme Court judges.

The problem in Brooklyn is not one or two individual villains, but the whole rotten, century-old system that mixes clubhouse politics and patronage with the majesty of the Constitution and the dignity of the law.

There are forty-six Supreme Court judges, each with a fourteen-year term, in the Brooklyn–Staten Island Judicial District. All but four were elected with the endorsement of both the Democratic and Republican parties. And more than half—including Rinaldi and Corso—were elected with the endorsement of three political parties.

The public never had a real voice in their election. And the legal profession never had a real voice in their nomination. All were nominated in judicial conventions, tightly controlled by district leaders, and all were elected in deals between party leaders that guaranteed no opposition. They are politicians picked for political reasons. They owe everything to the political organization. Legal excellence or distinction have little to do with the entire process. These judges can't even pick their own staff—the party organization does that.

In 1971, two Supreme Court judges were elected in Brooklyn; both had Democratic and Republican support. In 1970, six Supreme Court judgeships were open in Brooklyn. Five Democrats and one Republican were picked, and all six had bipartisan endorsement—and no serious opposition. In 1968, in the Brooklyn–Staten Island Judicial District, nineteen new judgeships were available, and all nineteen candidates received the endorsement of the Democratic, Republican, and Liberal parties.

There are $1 million worth of patronage jobs in the Brooklyn courts, and many of these jobs are controlled by a sixty-six-year-old mortician named James Mangano. Mangano has been a district leader in Red Hook since 1934 and has been general clerk and administrative director of the Brooklyn Supreme Court for two decades.

It is estimated that James Mangano personally controls about 150 jobs in the Brooklyn courts—judgeships, law secretaries, confidential attendants, clerks, court reporters, court officers, probation officers, and typists. Although he never went to law school, Mangano has made about ten of the current Supreme Court judges in Brooklyn.*

All but seven of Brooklyn's forty-six Democratic district leaders hold patronage jobs, most of them somewhere in the court system. Mangano is general clerk of the Supreme Court. Frank Cunningham, Jr., the district leader of Congressman John Rooney's home club, is chief clerk of the Supreme Court's Appellate Term in Brooklyn. Casper Fasullo, another powerful district leader, is a law assistant in the Surrogate's Court. District Leader Joseph Levine is a law secretary. District Leader Joseph Sciarra is also a law secretary.

In addition, the Republican state committeemen from seven different assembly districts hold patronage jobs in the Brooklyn courts, including Joseph Parisi, chief clerk of the Criminal Court; Nicholas Nittoly, deputy clerk of the Criminal Court; and Anthony Durso, clerk of the Supreme Court.

Such a rich and political court system has traditionally been a fertile ground for corruption, whether political contracts, personal favors, or organized crime payoffs. Maurice

---

* Mangano, a hard-line conservative on social issues, had his captains quietly working for Richard Nixon's re-election in 1972.

Nadjari, the governor's special prosecutor, summarized this way: "Our judges come up through political organizations and build up obligations along the way. At the same time, racketeers cultivate political figures, and when their people get into trouble, they try to use whatever influence they have. This influence is not going to be stopped completely until we separate justice from politics."

Meade Esposito, a former bail bondsman, has been county leader of Brooklyn since January, 1969. One day this fall, I had lunch with him in Foffe's Restaurant on Montague Street in Brooklyn and asked him about the courts. He spoke the word of reform, although the reader should be skeptical about anything a character like Esposito says. Esposito has a reputation for candor, but not truth.

"The whole system stinks," Esposito began. "The fourteen-year term for Supreme Court judges is too long. I'm for eight-year terms, and then let an impartial committee of lawyers and community people have the power to reappoint them every two years if they're doing a good job. If not, then get rid of them. But they should be reviewed every two years."

Esposito does not favor a direct primary for Supreme Court judges "because it would cost too much. If there was a primary, then all the judges would be rich boys from Harvard and Yale. I like some judges to come from Brooklyn College. And in this county you would never elect a member of a minority community to the court. This way we got someone like Tom Jones on the Supreme Court. . . .

"One reform I would favor is that every judge must live in his community. In Brooklyn we got a couple Supreme Court judges who moved right out to Long Island as soon as we made them. I want my judges to be involved in the life of the neighborhood. I want them in the clubhouses, where the people can see them. Not out in Riverhead someplace."

What about the practice of the party organization picking the law secretaries? Esposito believes in that kind of patronage. "What's wrong with the party appointing the law secretaries? You gotta reward the faithful. But I make sure they work, or else they're fired."

I asked Esposito about the generally low reputation of the courts and the appointment of Maurice Nadjari as the special prosecutor.

"Yeah, I'm in favor of the superseding DA. I know there's some decay in there. I say, let it fall wherever it falls. We have to clean it up. . . . Sure, there might be some contracts in the courts. But all this stuff about selling judgeships is a lot of crap. I defy anybody to say he gave me a dime for a judgeship."

What can you do about the bad judges?

"You prove something to me, and we'll get rid of them. There's one judge in Brooklyn Civil Court I'll tell you right now I will oppose for renomination—Ross Di Lorenzo. He's bad. He was district leader and nominated himself in 1964. I will tell all my leaders to dump him in 1974."

Each year a few good politicians deliver thoughtful speeches on the need for court reform. And then nothing happens.

In 1966 Robert Kennedy, campaigning to elect Sam Silverman the Manhattan surrogate, briefly ignited public interest in the cause of reform. Over the years Mayor Lindsay has made several excellent speeches calling for the appointment of all judges on a merit system, based on the recommendation of impartial screening committees. For the last two years, Lindsay has also proposed the creation of a permanent commission with a full-time staff to receive and investigate lawyer and citizen complaints against judges. Board of Correction Chairman William vanden Heuvel has also made many fine speeches listing most of the things that ought to be done to redeem the courts—greater productivity, stricter supervision, less political selection, better administration.

But reasonable, polite speeches do not transform powerful, self-important institutions like the courts. The years of accumulated rot in the court system require stronger remedies.

There is by now abundant evidence of terrible judgment, doubtful ethics, and probable corruption among some judges. The sentencing statistics collected by the Hughes Committee, the Knapp Commission report, continuing articles in the *Times* and the *Voice* have all helped expose to public scrutiny the essential facts of unequal justice. But no one seems willing to accept responsibility for taking the next step beyond exposure.

A critical newspaper article is hardly sufficient punishment for a judge who unnecessarily sends a heroin dealer back into this city's communities of suffering. A day's embarrassment is hardly an adequate deterrent to a judge who wants to accept a contract from the Mafia, which is, after all, the General Motors of the heroin business.

The time has finally come, I think, for the courts to clean their own house and remove judges like Dominic Rinaldi and Joseph Corso from their positions of immense power and prestige.

There are three possible mechanisms for removing judges. One is criminal indictment, which seems remote at this point, since there is no proof money changed hands in these cases.

A second possibility is impeachment by the state legislature. This also seems unlikely.

A third way, and the most plausible, would be to hold a trial on competency grounds by a judicial court. A judicial court can be convened by the Judicial Conference, which consists of all the administrative judges in the New York area. A judicial trial had been scheduled for Manhattan Supreme Court Judge Mitchell Schweitzer until Schweitzer resigned. I believe there is now a sufficient pattern of incompetent decisions by Judges Rinaldi and Corso to justify the rare spectacle of a judicial trial.

October 12, 1972

POSTSCRIPT

My view of how the average defendant is mistreated in the Brooklyn courts was supported by Federal Judge Orin Judd in a decision released on May 11, 1973.

Judge Judd's fifty-seven-page decision was in response to a class-action suit brought by the Legal Aid Society on behalf of all the inmates in the Brooklyn House of Detention.

Judge Judd wrote that the criminal parts of the courts in Brooklyn were "in a state of deep crisis. . . . The fault lies with the whole system. . . . It is evident that the overburdened, fragmented system used by Legal Aid has not measured up to the required constitutional level."

The decision also criticized Brooklyn judges for ignoring or rejecting motions made by inmates because no Legal Aid attorney was present. The Judd decision said, "The vast majority of *pro se* motions by inmates were not placed on court calendars, but remained in Legal Aid files."

Judge Judd, a Republican, is the same excellent jurist who saw that justice was done in the case of brutality by Deputy Warden Ossakow in the Kew Gardens jail.

Further confirmation of how the average litigant is screwed in the Brooklyn courts came in a sixty-two-page study of the Landlord-Tenant Parts in Brooklyn, released by the Junior League of Brooklyn on May 23, 1973.

This study, based on 1,029 cases during 1972, called the Landlord-Tenant Parts "a hellhole. . . . Only one-fourth of the tenants have lawyers to inform of the relevant law. . . . Cases observed were heard with difficulty because of shouting clerks and litigants. . . ."

The report also noted that "important records and documents are often missing or contradictory" and that judges themselves called the court a "fish market" and a "degrading place."

The report recommended that judges be monitored to "eliminate inappropriate manners"; that the court be kept open "till 5:00 P.M., instead of 3:00 P.M."; and that judges attend seminars to learn about new rent and housing laws.

The Politics
of Justice

THE New York City court system does not work.

Police Commissioner Patrick Murphy has said the courts cause rather than prevent crime. The courts are responsible for the terrible overcrowding of the jails. The courts keep the old-line political machines in business with patronage. And the courts do not administer justice equally.

Mafia members are five times more likely to win dismissals in the State Supreme Court than are other defendants, according to a study prepared by the Joint Legislative Committee on Crime. Heroin dealers are treated much more leniently by judges in Brooklyn than in any other borough. Poor people with court-appointed lawyers receive sentences twice as long for the same crime as citizens with enough money to hire their own attorneys.

More than 8,000 inmates are waiting for trials in New York City jails this week because they are too poor to make bail. The detention backlog in the State Supreme Court has increased from 3,518 to 5,836 in the last two years. In 1971, there were 94,000 felony arrests in New York City. Only 550 of those 94,000 actually went to trial.

CRUEL AND UNUSUAL JUSTICE

And somewhere, deep in the coils of this wounded city, I believe there is a connection between machine politics, organized crime, the heroin plague, the corruption of justice, and the rising crime rate. Short of exposing this ultimate root of corruption, the immediate objective should be the effort to separate law and justice from politics and patronage.

Right now, most sitting Supreme Court justices in this city were picked by politicians, for political reasons, without regard for ability or judicial qualifications. Many of the least qualified judges, like Al Lerner, Paul Fino, Ivan Warner, Francis X. Smith, Aaron Koota, and Joseph Corso, are former politicians. There are almost no State Supreme Court justices chosen on merit from the universities or from first-class law firms, where many of the better federal judges, like Jack Weinstein and Orin Judd, come from.

Having lost direct control of City Hall, the old political machines depend on the court system for most of their jobs; they could not survive without the judicial source of patronage. County leaders even insist on appointing the staffs of most Supreme Court justices. Influential district leaders like Duke Viggiano in Manhattan, Sam Tolisano in the Bronx, and Gerard Beldock in Brooklyn are law secretaries to Supreme Court justices. Viggiano's judge, Alfred Ascione, spends part of his time taking phone messages from politicians looking for his law secretary. Former Bronx Assemblyman Murray Lewinter is the law secretary to Supreme Court Justice Sullivan, even though he never passed the bar exam.

Almost all State Supreme Court justices are picked in secret negotiations among the county leaders and run with dual party endorsement; of the last ninety-seven Supreme Court justices, eighty-eight were elected with the support of both the Democrats and the Republicans. In 1972, half the Supreme Court candidates had the support of all four political parties.

All this means that judges are not independent; they owe their jobs to political machines and are subject to the influence of those machines. Cases or motions or appeals are usually fixed not with crude cash, but with a private phone call from the political leader who originally made the politician a judge. This also means that under the existing process, most judges are chosen without consideration for legal excellence and without public scrutiny. It may be called an election, but when a candidate is given both the Democratic and Republican endorsements, he is guaranteed a judge's robes. And since Supreme Court justices serve fourteen-year terms, with a tradition of automatic four-party renomination, they are on the bench for life without any accountability to the public.

The single worst influence in politicizing the court system has been Governor Nelson Rockefeller. The governor has the power to appoint members of the Court of Claims and to make interim appointments to the Supreme Court. Without exception, Rockefeller's appointments have been disgraceful.

One sitting Supreme Court justice told me: "Nelson thinks a judgeship is like a tip for voting right in Albany. He trades judgeships for votes in the legislature every session. He has hurt the court with every one of his appointments."

In 1971 Rockefeller needed two votes to pass his state

budget. Two conservative Queens assemblymen, Joe Kunzeman and Al Lerner, switched their votes at the last minute to pass the budget. At the close of the session, Rockefeller made sure both were rewarded with judgeships in part of the notorious package deal he worked out with Queens Democratic Leader Matt Troy. The Rockefeller-Troy deal split up nine judgeships, including six Supreme Court judgeships that the two major parties divided equally with dual endorsements.

As part of the same deal, Rockefeller secured a Queens Supreme Court judgeship for Republican Fred Hammer. Hammer was opposed by the City Bar Association because "he lacks judicial temperament." Despite this rare rebuke by the legal profession, Hammer was given the endorsement of all four political parties. He has proven to be a bigoted, abusive judge, and recently a group of antipoverty lawyers filed a formal complaint against him.

One morning in October, Hammer was sitting in the Matrimonial Part in Queens. At one point he asked a Legal Aid lawyer where he went to college. The lawyer told him Yale, and Judge Hammer asked, "Why is a smart kid like you wasting your time defending poor people?" A half hour later, Hammer began shouting at a nineteen-year-old black woman, telling her she should go out and get a job. The woman, who was seeking a divorce and was very nervous, broke into tears and ran out of the courtroom.

Still another piece of this same rotten Rockefeller-Troy deal was a Supreme Court judgeship for Queens State Senator Seymour Thaler. But Thaler was indicted and convicted of stealing U.S. Treasury bills, so he never made it to the bench.

Another Republican Supreme Court justice the governor is responsible for is Paul Fino of the Bronx. Fino was found unqualified by the Bar Association but was endorsed anyway by both the Republican and Democratic parties. Fino was the Supreme Court justice who, on May 26, 1972, ruled that landlords may legally charge tenants twice the 7.5 percent maximum increase provided under the 1970 rent law. Fino is now under investigation by a federal grand jury for allegedly accepting payoffs for introducing special immigration bills while he was a congressman.

Rockefeller's appointments to the Court of Claims have been total politics, with no regard for merit or ability. In 1963 Rockefeller appointed Republican party State Chairman Fred Young to the Court of Claims. A few months later Young resigned to help manage Rockefeller's 1964 presidential bid. When that failed, Rockefeller put Young back on the Court of Claims as the presiding judge in a maneuver so cynical it even offended the most pro-Rockefeller editorial writers and lawyers. At the 1967 State Constitutional Convention, Judge Young was the most free-spending lobbyist against court reform.

In April, 1971, Rockefeller made two Court of Claims appointments—Joseph Madugno and Louis Laurino. Modugno was a Conservative-Republican councilman from Queens; Laurino was chairman of Queens Democrats for Rockefeller during the 1970 gubernatorial campaign.

The City Bar Association judged Modugno unfit for the court. Modugno had practiced almost no courtroom law his entire working life. His only legal experience was processing workmen's compensation claims before referees. *The New*

York Times also editorialized against his nomination, saying it "degraded the courts."

Rockefeller then broke tradition and a promise by not even submitting Laurino's nomination for evaluation to the City Bar Association. Modugno is now sitting on the Court of Claims, adjudicating complex legal questions involving millions of dollars in citizens' negligence lawsuits against the state. He almost never rules against the state. Laurino is now the Queens surrogate as part of the Rockefeller-Troy deal.

Two other recent Rockefeller appointments to the Court of Claims were Frank Rossetti, Jr., the son of the Manhattan county leader, and Adolph Orlando, Fino's former law partner. Rossetti has turned out to be an adequate judge. But the point is, he got to be a judge only because of the power of his father. Orlando is notoriously inept.

Both the Surrogate's Court and the State Supreme Court are gold mines of patronage. Last year in Manhattan and Brooklyn alone, $1.9 million in receiverships and guardianships were given out to a narrow group of clubhouse lawyers, politicians, relatives of judges, and former judges. Good lawyers without political ties tend to be excluded from this form of patronage.

In 1969, for example, former Republican Assembly Speaker Joseph Carlino received an unprecedented $70,000 in court patronage. Last year Carlino also turned out to be the highest paid lobbyist in the state, receiving $90,000 from four clients, including the New York Racing Association and the Retail Merchants Association. One of Carlino's best friends, and the source of most of his patronage, is Manhattan Surrogate Sam DiFalco.

Other political insiders who received special guardianship appointments worth more than $1,000 from judges during 1969 included Robert Travia, the son of Federal Judge Anthony Travia; Irving Kirschenbaum, a former Republican assemblyman and now a Supreme Court justice; Sydelle Rinaldi, the wife of Brooklyn Supreme Court Justice Dominic Rinaldi; Joseph Cox, the retired Manhattan surrogate; Morris Eder, a former Supreme Court justice; Jonathan Weinstein, the son of Queens Supreme Court Justice Moe Weinstein; Congressman Mario Biaggi; Frank Rossetti, Jr., now a Court of Claims judge; and Bronx Councilman Bertram Gelfand, running for Bronx surrogate with the endorsement of all four parties.

Efforts to reform or abolish this lucrative system of patronage have been unsuccessful. It remains one of the basic ways the theoretically independent judiciary is used to support political machines and make them profitable for the bosses.

If the objective is to get politics out of the courts, there seem to be three possible methods of doing it.

One is to convince county leaders like Pat Cunningham, Meade Esposito, and Matt Troy voluntarily to surrender their immense judge-making powers to impartial committees of lawyers and community leaders (this has been done in Manhattan). These panels would then interview aspirants and recommend judicial candidates on the basis of merit. Some of the county leaders have praised this method in the abstract but have done nothing to implement it.

The second possibility is to have all judges appointed by an independent nominating commission. This makes sense because the essential point is that judges should be independent rather than representative. It is the legislative and executive branches of government that must be representative. (A strong argument against elected judges is Sol Wachtler's lavishly financed campaign for the Court of Appeals.) The current system permits the county leaders to control the State Supreme Court through deals that make a mockery of the electoral process.

The third alternative, also necessary, is a renewed effort to break the remaining political machines in this city.

Not all judges who come out of the clubhouses are bad. Some, like Irwin Brownstein, Vincent Damiani, and David Ross, are very good. But the most incompetent judges are all creations of the political machines or the governor.

Brooklyn Supreme Court Justice Dominic Rinaldi is a typical machine judge. Rinaldi is also one of the most powerful judges in Brooklyn. He was first elevated to the bench by John Sharkey in 1960; since then, both Stanley Steingut and Meade Esposito have been helpful to him. In 1965, Esposito arranged for Rinaldi's appointment to the Temporary Study Commission on the Courts, a prestige prize many fine judges wanted.

Another measure of Rinaldi's power is that he is assigned part of the year to Suffolk County. This is a favor to Rinaldi. George Aspland, the Suffolk district attorney, has asked that Rinaldi not sit in Suffolk, but his request has been ignored. The presumption is that Rinaldi has influential friends outside the court system.

Brooklyn Supreme Court Justice Joseph Corso is another typical creation of the county leaders. He was an assemblyman for sixteen years and a Civil Court judge for two years;

in 1968, Brooklyn County Leader Stanley Steingut promoted Corso to the Supreme Court. In the last eighteen months, Corso has thrown the indictments of five different Mafiosi out of court, and all five have been unanimously reinstated by the Appellate Division.

Queen Supreme Court Justice Albert Bosch is still another judge who made it within the traditional clubhouse structure. Two years ago he allowed a police detective named Joseph DeVito, upon a felony charge, to plead guilty to a misdemeanor, and then let him off with a suspended sentence.

There can no longer be any question of romanticizing organized crime. The Mafia is deep into the heroin business, and the enormous profits from the economy of junk are the reason mobsters kill each other. But it is junkies who cause most of the street crimes that terrorize people—muggings, stickups, assaults. And it is the ghettos that suffer most. The Mafia takes more money—$51 million a year—out of Bedford-Stuyvesant with illegal heroin, prostitution, and gambling operations, than the federal government takes out in taxes.

A thoughtful and original study of organized crime in Brooklyn's 77th and 79th Precincts completed by Jerry McKenna, of the staff of the Joint Legislative Committee on Crime, and Harold Lasswell, a political scientist and former Yale law professor, provide some provocative data. The McKenna-Lasswell paper analyzed sixty-two felony narcotics arrests made between January, 1969, and October, 1971, in Bedford-Stuyvesant. Of those arrested, 52 percent won dismissals from Brooklyn judges, 7 percent were placed on probation, 3 percent were discharged, 7 percent jumped bail, 18 percent had not yet been sentenced, and only 13 percent went to prison.

So breaking the political machine might be more than just good government. It might also be a contribution toward solving the most frightening problem in this city today —the fear of crime and violence.

November 9, 1972

HOW PATRONAGE WORKS

MANHATTAN

NAME	POLITICAL AFFILIATION	POSITION IN COURT SYSTEM
P. Vincent (Duke) Viggiano	Democratic Leader	Law Secretary to Judge Ascione
Guy Vellella	Republican candidate for assembly in Bronx	Law Secretary to Judge Kirschenbaum
Nathan Ravner	Officer in Democratic Club	Law Secretary to Judge Nadel
Marion Stone	Democratic Leader	Confidential Attendant to Judge Ascione
David Stein	President of Democratic Club	Confidential Attendant to Judge Mangan
Ann Rode	Democratic Leader	Confidential Attendant to Judge Riccobono
Morris Solomon	Officer of Democratic Club	Law Secretary to Judge Postel (Solomon is not a lawyer)

MANHATTAN

NAME	POLITICAL AFFILIATION	POSITION IN COURT SYSTEM
Geraldine Daniels	Democratic State Committee-woman	Confidential Attendant to Judge Culkin
Marion Weinstein	Democratic Leader	Confidential Attendant
Gil Rosa	Officer and Member, Board of Governors, East Side Republican Club	Deputy County Clerk
Joseph Velardi	Officer in Republican Club	Referee

THE BRONX

NAME	POLITICAL AFFILIATION	POSITION IN COURT SYSTEM
Samuel Tolisano	Democratic Leader	Secretary to Judge Brust
Mildred Klett	Democratic Executive Committee	Confidential Attendant to Judge Brust
Sylvia Liebman	Democratic Leader	Confidential Attendant to Judge Dollinger
Samuel Adelson	President of Democratic Club	Secretary to Judge Helman
Gerard Esposito	Democratic Leader	Secretary to Judge Kapelman
Ethel Frank	Democratic Leader	Confidential Attendant to Judge Korn
Stephen Carbone	Democratic Leader	Confidential Attendant to Judge McCaffrey

THE BRONX

NAME	POLITICAL AFFILIATION	POSITION IN COURT SYSTEM
Murray Lewinter	Democratic Leader	Secretary to Judge Sullivan
Cecilia Heller	Democratic Executive Committee	Confidential Attendant to Judge Tierney
John Whalen	Democratic Leader	Captain–Court Officer, Supreme Court
Sue Ginsburg	Democratic Leader	Deputy County Clerk
Julia Cargiulo	Democratic Leader	Deputy County Clerk
Rose Catania	Democratic Executive Committee	General Clerk's Office
John J. Sullivan	Democratic Executive Committee	Chief Clerk, Bronx Surrogate
Thomas O'Brien	Democratic Leader	Secretary to Judge Sullivan
Stephen Kaufman	Democratic State Committee	Secretary to Judge Cohen
Jerome Glanzrock	Democratic Leader	Assistant Court Clerk (Exempt), Civil Court
Peggy Bernheim	Democratic State Committee	Law Secretary to Judge Louis Peck, Civil
Thomas Galligan	President of Democratic Club	Supreme Court
Julia Madden	Democratic State Committee	Secretary to County Clerk
Howard Tyson	Democratic Executive Committee	Chief Clerk, Civil Court

Seven Suspicious
Cases

THE FIRST TIME I saw Manhattan Supreme Court Justice Gerald Culkin was the day he ordered WBAI's general manager, Ed Goodman, to jail for contempt of court.

Goodman, invoking New York's broad newsman's confidentiality statute, refused to turn over to the district attorney thirty hours of tapes made during the Tombs uprising of October, 1970. In a similar case involving the *Voice,* no one was going to jail. So I was a little shocked when Justice Culkin sentenced Goodman to thirty days, refusing to grant bail, refusing to permit Goodman to make a statement to the court, refusing even to delay sentence until after lunch.

I mentally labeled Culkin as just another conservative, repressive judge and forgot about him. Then, three months later, on June 15, the Joint Legislative Committee on Crime held a public hearing that explored the anatomy of four felony narcotics cases in which the judge gave inexplicably permissive sentences to heroin dealers. One of the four justices named by police detectives that day was Gerald Culkin. As a result of this generosity toward dealers of death, as contrasted to the harshness toward a listener-owned, anti-establishment radio station, I began to investigate other decisions and dispositions made by Justice Culkin.

What I have discovered, after several months of research, is not only a history of leniency toward heroin dealers, but also a history of leniency toward the Mafia and toward cops and politicians charged with corruption.

Justice Culkin's permissiveness with dealers, mobsters, and crooked cops is highly suspicious because so many of his decisions in specific cases had no legal foundation and were later unanimously reversed by the Appellate Division.

Justice Culkin has also been the object of an unusual public rebuke from Manhattan District Attorney Frank Hogan, who almost never criticizes a judge by name to the media. The case that so disturbed Hogan involved Police Lieutenant Francis X. Ward, who was indicted on four counts of perjury and contempt by a grand jury investigating police corruption by organized crime. Justice Culkin dismissed the indictment against Ward on the most flimsy legal grounds. And Hogan said: "Justice Culkin either misread the record, or chooses to ignore it. . . . His decision is vague, illogical, misleading, and grossly unfair to the people."

Hogan appealed Culkin's ruling and it was unanimously reversed by a higher court.

Justice Culkin's closest friend is a lawyer named Joseph Aronstein. Both men are officers of the Tough Club, a private social club at 243 West 14th Street. Along with Culkin's law secretary, Joe Mariconda (who never went to law school or college), the two men can be seen dining together and playing cards several nights a week at the Tough Club. Aronstein has a very sleazy reputation among his fellow lawyers. He has been indicted twice—but never convicted—for bribery. And for years he has specialized in defending Mafia members. Every time he has argued a writ or a motion by a Mafioso before his friend Justice Culkin, he has won a favorable decision. Most lawyers and jurists believe it is clearly unethical for Culkin even to hear cases involving Aronstein.

Joseph Gentile is listed by police as a member of the Profaci organized crime family. He was indicted in June, 1962, for operating a policy bank. On July 27, 1962, Gentile's lawyer, Joseph Aronstein, filed a motion before Justice Culkin to dismiss the charges against his client. Aronstein's grounds were that the search warrant was improperly drawn.

A similar technical motion against the search warrant was also filed by Gentile's codefendants before Justice Mitchell Schweitzer. On September 17, 1962, the same day on which the validity and legality of the search warrant was upheld by Justice Schweitzer, Justice Culkin found the same warrant defective and dismissed the indictment against Aronstein's client. The basis for Justice Culkin's decision was that the search warrant did not contain a statement limiting the time period for its execution and was therefore invalid. The warrant had been executed the same day it was issued.

Justice Culkin also threw out the indictment without having read the grand jury minutes. The minutes of the grand jury proceedings had not even been transcribed when Culkin granted Aronstein's motion to dismiss.

In 1964, the Appellate Division unanimously reversed Justice Culkin's decision. The defendant, Joseph Gentile, subsequently pleaded guilty.

Samuel Kass was convicted of selling heroin on December 6, 1951. On May 7, 1968, Aronstein submitted to Justice Culkin a petition for a writ of error *coram nobis* on behalf of Kass. This same writ had been submitted by other lawyers to other judges on many previous occasions and had been rejected each time without a hearing.

The substance of Aronstein's petition was that his client had been coerced by the district attorney to accept a plea, and this was done in the presence of his prior lawyer, Sol Gelb. This was the same point made in all the other rejected petitions. No new evidence was offered. Justice Culkin nevertheless ordered a hearing on Aronstein's motion.

According to the transcript of the hearing, Kass testified that Sol Gelb had *not* been present when he was allegedly coerced to plead guilty. Confronted with the contrary claim in his sworn petition of May 7, 1968, Kass quickly reversed himself and testified that his attorney had been present at the plea-bargaining session. Gelb then testified that Kass was not telling the truth and that at no time was his former client threatened or intimidated by the DA in his presence. Despite this, Justice Culkin granted Aronstein's writ and vacated the conviction of heroin-seller Sam Kass.

The Appellate Division unanimously reversed Justice Culkin's order and reinstated the conviction of Kass.

David Betillo has been described by law enforcement agencies as "Lucky Luciano's chief deputy." In 1936 Betillo was convicted, after a sensational trial, on sixty-two counts of compulsory prostitution. He was sentenced to not fewer than twenty-five and not more than forty years in prison.

On March 24, 1966, upon the application of Betillo's attorney, Joseph Aronstein, Justice Culkin issued a writ of habeas corpus, returnable in Manhattan. At the time, Betillo was back in prison for violation of parole.

Hogan's office appealed Culkin's decision, arguing that under the law the writ should be returnable in the county where Betillo was being detained—Dutchess County—and not in Manhattan. Hogan's fear was that if Betillo and Aronstein managed to appear before Justice Culkin, they were sure to win.

The Court of Appeals reversed Justice Culkin's decision —unanimously.

Justice Culkin's good friend, lawyer Joseph Aronstein, had his trial for bribery in October in Manhattan before Supreme Court Justice Andrew Tyler. Aronstein was acquitted of trying to bribe a policeman, Ed Patterson, who is assigned to the 70th Precinct in Brooklyn.

Before the trial was even over, Patrolman Patterson called me up and said, "I'm afraid this case is fixed against me." Patterson explained that he had made a tape of Aronstein's attempt to bribe him and that Justice Tyler had refused to admit as evidence a transcript of that tape, although he permitted the barely audible tape to be played.

After Aronstein was acquitted, I spoke to an assistant district attorney close to Manhattan DA Frank Hogan. This aide told me: "Justice Tyler should be investigated by a Court on the Judiciary for the way he handled the Aronstein trial. He was obviously biased for the defendant. He gave a totally biased charge to the jury. He ruled crucial evidence was inadmissible. His hostility to the prosecution was apparent in every ruling he made from the bench."

Last year Justice Andrew Tyler was under active investigation by Hogan's office in connection with the misappropriation of antipoverty funds in Harlem. Other law enforcement officials have become suspicious of the fact that Justice Tyler has been visiting the office of an important bail bondsman on Baxter Street. This is regarded as highly questionable conduct for a sitting Supreme Court justice. And several agencies are now looking into his handling of the Aronstein trial.

On December 2, 1970, after a month-long investigation, police obtained a search warrant to enter the apartment of Gloria Cannon in Harlem. There, police found eight pounds of cocaine and heroin. Gloria Cannon was receiving welfare but was immediately able to post a $25,000 bail bond. It seemed clear she was part of a major narcotics distribution system.

Gloria Cannon's trial for a Class A narcotics felony was held before Justice Culkin. Toward the end of the trial, the defendant changed her mind and pleaded guilty to a Class B felony. Under the law, Justice Culkin could have sentenced the defendant to twenty-five years. Instead, Culkin gave her one to three years, and she is now free.

In 1959, former Manhattan Borough President Hulan Jack was indicted for conspiracy and accepting gratuities. On March 15, 1960, Justice Culkin dismissed the indictment on minor technical grounds that seemed ludicrous to most lawyers. In his dismissal order, for example, Justice Culkin claimed the indictment was invalid because it did not say Jack knew Sidney Ungar had business dealings with the city government.

On April 21, 1960, the Appellate Division, in a lengthy opinion, unanimously overruled Justice Culkin's dismissal and reinstated the original indictment. That reversal was unanimously affirmed by the Court of Appeals on May 26, 1960. These two rulings by higher courts meant that twelve different appellate judges had found no legal or constitutional evidence to justify Culkin's effort to save Hulan Jack from going to trial.

Culkin, like Hulan Jack, was a creation of the Tammany machine, and both were close friends of Carmine De Sapio. Culkin's father had been a powerful Tammany leader, and Culkin got his judgeship originally through the influence of his father in the Manhattan organization.

On January 16, 1961, Hulan Jack was found guilty, and that verdict was affirmed by both the Appellate Division and the Court of Appeals.

In the last eighteen months, Justice Culkin has dismissed indictments in two cases of police corruption in decisions that stunned the legal world because they seemed so bereft of judicial merit. In one case, Culkin's decision was reversed unanimously. The second occurred only recently, and will be appealed by the district attorney.

On July 30, 1970, Police Lieutenant Francis X. Ward was indicted on four counts of perjury and contempt by a grand jury investigating police corruption. Lieutenant Ward, testifying under a grant of immunity, had admitted to the grand jury that while he was assigned to the police commissioner's Confidential Investigating Unit he had accepted money to protect the notorious bookmaker Hugh Mulligan from prosecution. Later, however, Ward made conflicting statements to the grand jury about how much money he had taken.

On February 22, 1971, Justice Culkin dismissed the indictment against Lieutenant Ward. Justice Culkin, in his remarkable decision, threw out the perjury counts because they were "somewhat vague," and the witness was "confused."

District Attorney Hogan then called in the press and, for the first time in ten years, criticized a sitting Supreme Court justice by name for a decision. On appeal, Culkin's decision was unanimously reversed. Ward was tried and convicted, and on March 27, 1973, he was sentenced to up to three years by Supreme Court Justice Peter McQuillan.

In mid-October, Justice Culkin, in another case of high-level police corruption by organized crime, threw out the indictments of two former detectives, Andrew Dunleavy and Martin Zincand. They had been indicted for allegedly lying to a grand jury investigating a complex case involving a homicide and a major heroin dealer. In his decision, Justice Culkin explained the two former detectives were not lying, but were "confused."

The lawyers for Dunleavy and Zincand had filed their motion the previous May, during a week when Justice Culkin was sitting in Part 30 of the Supreme Court. After the Ward decision, Hogan had made a formal request to Presiding Justice Stevens that Culkin not be assigned to the

Motion Part because he had handed down so many dubious decisions there. Nevertheless, Culkin was back in Part 30 that May, and the lawyers timed their appeal to his assignment there.

Culkin sat on the motion for six months before he dismissed it. And he did not send a copy of his decision to the *Law Journal,* something highly unusual in such a significant case.

A bureau chief in Hogan's office called this latest Culkin dismissal "incredible and frankly suspicious."

There is, it should be pointed out, another side to the story of Justice Culkin.

Even the judge's severest critics point out that Culkin is a kind, sensitive person. He is not normally cruel or abusive to defendants, the way other incompetent judges like Dominic Rinaldi or Aaron Koota are. He does not give excessive prison sentences to young black addicts, the way Paul Fino does.

One assistant district attorney told me: "Culkin is a strange bird. I believe he accepts contracts on many cases, but he probably doesn't take money. He does it out of some twisted code of loyalty to his old clubhouse cronies or to personal friends like Joe Aronstein. Culkin is a rich guy. He doesn't need any money. Maybe he just likes to play the big shot with a bad bunch of people. I think he should be impeached, but I will say for him that at least he doesn't try to make up for his leniency on some people by taking it out on poor blacks. There are some judges who, when they don't have a contract, will try to clean up their reputation by giving some poor junkie twenty years. But Culkin won't do that. He's a nice man, but there is no question that he should have been kicked off the bench ten years ago."

This shade of ambiguity about Culkin is supported by a famous tape made by Manhattan District Leader Charles Kinsolving in 1966, when a lawyer named Gussie Kleinman approached Kinsolving to seek his support for Culkin. At the time, Culkin, who remained very political even as a judge, was trying to generate enough backing to run for Manhattan surrogate. The tape shows the lawyer telling Kinsolving: "Culkin has always been a party man. If somebody from the club comes before him, he will find law to support him. . . . Because some of his decisions look so radical, they figure he must have gotten something for it. But it's not true at all. Because he wouldn't make those decisions if he was really taking. You know what I mean? First of all he doesn't need the dough. But I would say this—if you come in front of him, and you're a friend of his, he'll bend over backwards to find law to support you."

Kinsolving did not support Culkin for surrogate that year.*

In the last year it has become clear there is a staggering amount of corruption within the entire criminal justice system in New York City. In the first ten months of 1972, more than eighty policemen were arrested on corruption charges, and thirty-one other cops were suspended for suspected graft and payoffs. The chief of the Grand Jury Bureau in Queens DA Tom Mackell's office has been indicted for splitting a $15,000 bribe with a prominent bail bondsman

---

* For additional insight into the ethics of Judge Culkin, see *The Washington Pay-off* by Robert Winter-berger, pp. 142 and 146.

and a Queens criminal lawyer. A half dozen other members of Mackell's staff are now under investigation by a federal grand jury in Brooklyn. Manhattan Supreme Court Justice Mitchell Schweitzer was forced to quit under considerable evidence of corruption. Special State Prosecutor Maurice Nadjari has said he is now investigating "more than twenty judges" for possible corruption. And a week ago, Detective Nicholas Lamattina and admitted judge-fixer Nicholas De Stefano pleaded guilty in federal court to trying to bribe undercover narcotics detective Robert Leucci in order to get access to secret files in the office of the U.S. attorney.

Meanwhile, the Knapp Commission report and the annual report of the State Commission of Investigation both concluded there was "widespread corruption" among cops, prosecutors, and judges.

This level of discovered corruption in one year in New York City is frightening. It suggests that organized crime and the major heroin dealers are flourishing because they can purchase protection. An incorruptible criminal justice system seems a precondition for any hope of coping with the rising plague of street crime and narcotics addiction. As long as the dealer or the mobster can buy immunity, there can be neither justice nor safety.

Such a massive scale of corruption destroys both respect for law and confidence in government. If it becomes folk wisdom that cops are on the pad and judges take contracts, the result is the casual cynicism that prevents any outrage over the ITT scandal or the Watergate scandal. We just assume everyone is crooked, including the president.

A few people seem willing to do something about improving the administration of justice in New York. Bob

Morgenthau did something when he was U.S. attorney; the late John Hughes, chairman of the Joint Legislative Committee on Crime, was a model of how a serious conservative might preserve law and justice. David Durk and Frank Serpico are heroes. Police Commissioner Patrick Murphy, Bronx DA Burt Roberts, and Brooklyn DA Eugene Gold have shown how we can combat the corruption of justice. But one powerful group is doing nothing about the problem —the presiding justices responsible for supervising the court system.

Samuel Rabin is presiding justice of the Appellate Division for the Second Department (Brooklyn, Queens, Staten Island, and the suburbs). Harold Stevens is the presiding justice for the First Department (Manhattan and the Bronx). And Stanley Fuld is the chief judge of the Court of Appeals, the senior jurist in the state. Outside the legal profession these three men, all over sixty-five years old, are almost unknown. But they are the accountable rulers of the judicial system. Reporter Lesley Oelsner described their mystique well in a *Times* article in April, 1972: "Aides speak to them in hushed voices, and about them in reverent phrases. Lawyers address them politely, and even obsequiously. . . . Let them walk into a courtroom, and both the clerk at the bar, and the judge at the bench, straighten up at once."

Whenever the courts are criticized, the two "PJs"—Rabin and Stevens—are the first to defend the status quo. They are supreme examples of the club mentality. Whenever Mayor Lindsay or William vanden Heuvel has made reasonable and constructive suggestions for reform, the PJs have counterattacked. When the cautious and conservative Frank

Hogan rebuked Justice Culkin for his dismissal of the Ward case, Stevens's reaction was to attack Hogan in the press. The PJs have not displayed the slightest initiative in disciplining or removing incompetent judges. Their attitude of passivity and defensiveness is in sharp contrast to the sense of urgency of Police Commissioner Murphy.

The mountain of corruption around Manhattan Supreme Court Justice Schweitzer was first leaked to the press by the late John Hughes only because he was so frustrated by the indifference of Chief Judge Fuld. Senator Hughes had spent several weeks trying to get Judge Fuld to read the evasive and incriminating transcript of Justice Schweitzer's executive session testimony. Finally, when Judge Fuld told Hughes he might read the transcript after he finished reading *War and Peace,* Hughes went straight to *The New York Times* the next morning.

And when the evidence of corruption became public, Justice Schweitzer was permitted to resign quietly like a gentleman, with his full pension of $25,000 a year.

Recently, in a revealing response to all the problems in the judiciary, the Board of Judges hired Ruder & Finn, the second largest public relations firm on Madison Avenue, to improve the image of the courts. Meanwhile, substantial evidence of judicial misconduct has been offered in the pages of the *Voice.* Mary Perot Nichols reported how Brooklyn Civil Court Judge Ross Di Lorenzo took the Fifth Amendment before a federal grand jury on whether he tried to fix a case involving organized crime. Nichols also reported that Judge Di Lorenzo lied four times at a hearing before a court referee looking into the same case, only to change his testimony when confronted with the grand jury minutes. Di

Lorenzo is still a judge in Brooklyn, thanks to the permissive Appellate Division.

Previously I reported that Brooklyn Supreme Court Justice Dominic Rinaldi gave an illegal conditional discharge (no time in jail) to a heroin dealer named Clifton Glover.

This was illegal. Section 65.01 (1) of the Penal Law prohibits the imposition of the sentence of a conditional discharge for any narcotics felony. And, according to the Police Department and the district attorney, Glover provided no information on higher-ups in the heroin traffic to justify the extraordinary leniency granted him.

I have also described five different cases in which Brooklyn Supreme Court Justice Joseph Corso dismissed indictments against Mafia members; all five were later reversed by the Appellate Division. Corso has now been questioned by a grand jury about one of those five cases, the one in which Vincent De Cicco, an alleged member of the Carlo Gambino family, was given a much lighter sentence by Justice Corso than the Probation Department had recommended. Despite this active grand jury investigation, according to one law enforcement official, Justice Rabin has not begun his own inquiry into any of the five suspicious cases.

These are serious charges against Judges Di Lorenzo, Rinaldi, and Corso. If they were being made about a cop or a sanitation worker, there would be an immediate investigation by those in authority. But Presiding Justice Rabin, who is responsible for discipline and supervision of the Brooklyn courts, seems indifferent.

The same can be said of Presiding Justice Stevens and these seven curious cases involving Justice Culkin in Manhattan. Even if it turns out there is no criminal corruption, there are serious questions of ethics and competence about all four of these judges. And ethics and competence are both possible grounds for removal.

The judiciary is not a closed club of gentlemen. It is a public trust. The time has come when those who are accountable must clean their own house and restore public confidence in the administration of justice in this city.

November 30, 1972

There have been periodic campaigns to clean up the judiciary throughout the history of New York City. One of the last major efforts came during the early 1950s, when evidence of Mafia influence and bought judgeships came out during the Kefauver Committee's hearings and in the report of the State Crime Commission.

What follows is an excerpt from a pamphlet published by the Citizens Union in 1953 that called for the appointment of all judges as a means of stopping clubhouse domination of the judiciary. The CU pamphlet, I think, provides a valuable sense of continuity and history to the current campaign to clean up and depoliticize the court system.

Who Picks Our Judges?

The newspapers here pay scant attention to judicial contests —there are too many such affairs within their great 10-county scope—and the voters have nothing to go by except a blind and unconfident faith in the party label which is there on the voting machine to guide their uncritical fingers. A canvass of any hundred voters as they hurry away from the polls would disclose that 90 percent of them could not offer any reason for their votes for a judge beyond that party label! And would indeed have difficulty in recalling the names of the candidates they had just voted for for the judicial posts!

In New York City getting judges by election does not work—it fails to obtain any real verdict from the voters.

Here is how it *does* work—at least sometimes—hot from the griddle of the State Crime Commission, whose Second Report of last March is the richest and most fascinating picture of our politics ever written. We condense:

"A former assistant U.S. Attorney testified that District Leader William J. Connolly offered him the Democratic nomination in 1947 for Municipal Court Justice for $15,000 plus $10,-000 for campaign expenses. Analysis of Connolly's finances revealed that in 1947, 1948, and 1949, he spent $10,000 more than the receipts he could account for. He received, for his club, contributions from underworld sources.

"District Leader Simonetti, according to evidence corroborated in part by District Leader Jones, suggested to a prospective candidate for Municipal Court Justice that the probable 'expenses' would be $15,000 to $20,000 and to another that the cost would amount to $100 for each of some 182 election districts.

"District Leader Moses, also in 1948–49 secretary of the county organization and till recently secretary to a judge at $5200, admitted friendships with known criminals and activities in their behalf; when asked to explain expenditures beyond his visible income he took refuge in the bar against self-incrimination.

"District Leader Kantor admitted prior perjury, close friendship with underworld characters, and that he owes one of them several thousand dollars without note, interest, or security.

"The foregoing were all Democrats who continued in their leaderships after these disclosures, though all but one have since been displaced.

"Republican District Leader Fanelli admitted he and another leader, Rose, were partly instrumental in nominating Judge Matteo, whereafter Rose became the judge's clerk. When Rose resigned, Fanelli's brother got the job. Fanelli himself is secretary to another judge.

"Republican Bronx County Leader Knewitz, also a district leader for 40 years, living a charmed life in a sinecure court commissionership by the grace of the Bronx Democratic machine, testified that district leaders and their precinct captains consistently picked the hordes of committeemen by whom they were subsequently re-elected and also picked the long slates of delegates to the judicial conventions, which never in his experience had failed to adopt the leader's choice for judgeship nominees.

"Former Democratic County Leader Loughlin, current district leader Bert Stand, and the current County Leader De Sapio confirmed the practice and their unbroken power to deliver judicial nominations equivalent to election, the county leaders doing as they pleased with county and bi-county judges and the district leaders in the appropriate groupings agreeing on the judges for certain intra-county judicial districts.

"Out of 199 leaders in both parties January 1952, 57 (29 per cent) were then employed in the courts. In a list of 76 such current or recent positions only 26 were lawyers."

All that is condensed from the Crime Commission Report No. 2.

In October, 1953, the Civil Service Reform Association counted 62 district leaders and their close relatives in exempt court positions.

To summarize:

1. Judges are awarded party nominations by district or county leaders whose selections are final despite the folderol of subsequent party primaries, judicial conventions, and November elections.

2. Judges, thus chosen, often turn around and reward district leaders or their relatives and political cronies with sinecure jobs as clerks and secretaries exempt from civil service tests.

3. Some of these district leaders associate with criminals and are tough characters themselves; they ought not be the persons who award to judicial aspirants party nominations which are frequently equivalent to election.

It's hackneyed now; but recall Mr. Aurelio, who in 1943 was caught telephoning his "undying gratitude" to gambler Frank Costello for his nomination. Costello went out of circulation, but Aurelio is on the bench today! It was found impossible to get enough public attention to that tell-tale incident in a secondary contest amid the pandemonium of a big election. It came out too late to permit getting his name off the ballot. The leaderships of both parties promptly withdrew their sponsorships and publicly besought their party members to give Aurelio no votes, but a great unawareness remained and 50 percent of the Republicans and 73 percent of the Democrats followed the party labels and put him into office.

No—the method of selecting judges by popular election sounds all right but it does not work well enough in our metropolitan hurlyburly. And 100 years is a long enough trial.

It gives us too many mediocre judges—it gives us judges chosen mainly from the five percent of lawyers who are friends of politicians and who have been serviceable to politicians.

It is a wonder that the results are not worse and that so many judges and so many of the party leaders who choose them are as honest as any of us. But it's a loose and leaky system!

And now, with the fresh proofs of the Crime Commission in hand, is our chance to change.

POSTSCRIPT

In March of 1973, the Appellate Division overruled Culkin's dismissal of the indictments against Andrew Dunleavy and Martin Zincund. This marked the eighth time that a higher court had upheld DA Hogan's appeals of Culkin's rulings in cases involving official corruption or organized crime.

In June of 1973, another decision of Judge Culkin's was reversed by the Appellate Division that merits notice here. The case involved Otis Donald Harris. The state of South Carolina sought the extradition of an Otis *John* Harris, and Otis Donald appeared before Justice Culkin, who ordered his extradition after a brief hearing. The Appellate Division overruled Culkin's decision—unanimously—"on the law and the facts, and in the interest of justice."

The Appellate Division pointed out that the defendant had produced in court a certified birth certificate showing his name was Otis *Donald* Harris. The decision went on to say:

After the People concluded their case, the following colloquy took place:

"The Court: All right, the writ is dismissed.

"Mr. Wojswilo [Mr. Harris's lawyer]: Your honor, I am not finished.

"The Court [Judge Culkin]: As far as I'm concerned, you're finished.

"Mr. Wojswilo: Mr. Harris would like to take the stand.

"The Court: Put it on the record. Dismissed."

In view of the truncated nature of the hearing, in which relator was apparently curtailed from presenting his full proof . . . a right sense of justice mandates a new hearing.

The Life and
Hard Times of
Judge Aaron Koota

THREE separate law enforcement agencies are looking into Judge Aaron Koota's handling of a heroin case in the Brooklyn Supreme Court earlier this year.

The defendant in the case was Ira Karl Isaacs, an important heroin dealer in Bedford-Stuyvesant who obtained his narcotics from organized crime wholesalers. Isaacs was arrested on June 4, 1971, for possession of heroin. At the time of his arrest, Isaacs was on probation for selling heroin. His previous record of convictions included two for drug-related forgeries, two for possession of drugs, and one for the sale of heroin, for which he received a conditional discharge. In addition, the last time he had been arrested Isaacs had had three guns.

On March 2, 1972, Isaacs had a hearing before Judge Aaron Koota in the Brooklyn Supreme Court. His lawyer was Brooklyn Councilman Rudy Di Blasi, who had worked for Koota when Koota was district attorney of Brooklyn.

Two weeks before the hearing, Koota told Marty Hershy, the chief of the Narcotics Bureau in District Attorney Gold's office, that he was going to throw out the indictment against Isaacs because of a technical error in the search warrant.

According to the official court transcript of the March 2 hearing, Councilman Di Blasi made a motion to suppress evidence on the basis of an insufficient search warrant. Judge Koota immediately granted the motion.

Prosecutor Hershy then pointed out that under the law there must be a hearing with witnesses before Judge Koota can make such a decision. At that point, Judge Koota admitted his legal error and acknowledged there must be a formal hearing, that he could not legally dismiss the indictment merely on the basis of the written briefs.

Hershy then made a motion for Judge Koota to disqualify himself from the case, pointing out that the judge had already made up his mind since he'd said two weeks earlier that he was going to throw the case out of court.

Infuriated, Koota denied the motion to disqualify himself, and then reversed his earlier ruling, claiming there did not have to be a hearing and saying he was now dismissing the indictment against Isaacs on the grounds of a faulty search warrant.

Brooklyn District Attorney Eugene Gold appealed Koota's decision to the Appellate Division. In early November the Appellate Division, ruling unanimously that Koota was in error, reinstated the original indictment against Isaacs. Five appellate judges found the search warrant to be "legally more than sufficient."

According to another judge who knows the details of the

case: "That search warrant was as good as any ever written in Brooklyn. Everyone in the courthouse smelled something fishy in the Isaacs case."

According to a source within one of the law enforcement agencies studying the Isaacs transcript, "There are at least three other cases involving either narcotics or organized crime where we feel that Judge Koota's decisions are suspicious because they are unsupported by either law or logic."

Aaron Koota was district attorney of Brooklyn from 1964 to 1968. By any standard, he was one of the worst DAs in recent history. When he ran for DA in 1965, both the *Times* and the *Herald Tribune* opposed his election.

Part of Koota's 1965 campaign was the circulation of 500,000 brochures warning parents against child molesters. Koota's picture was on the cover of the brochure, which was supposed to be nonpolitical and educational. After the campaign was over, Koota admitted that the cost of printing and distributing the brochure was underwritten by Brooklyn banks.

Koota ran his office in a purely political fashion. All the assistant DAs came out of the political clubhouses, and all of them had to be approved by the county leader, Assemblyman Stanley Steingut. It was a useful source of patronage for Steingut, and it was Steingut who arranged for Koota's undeserved Supreme Court judgeship at the 1968 judicial convention. (It was also Steingut who arranged, at the same time, for Joseph Corso to become a Supreme Court Justice.)

Merit and ability and integrity had nothing to do with

the method Koota had used to staff his office. Under Koota, the assistant DAs were permitted to practice law on the side. This meant the courts closed after lunch, when most DAs went to work for their private clients.

In sharp contrast, Koota's successor as Brooklyn DA, Eugene Gold, advertised publicly for assistants in the *Law Journal* when he took over the office in 1969. Gold visited sixteen law schools recruiting the best talent he could find and taking no recommendations from the county leader. In one year, Gold reduced the average age of the assistants in the Brooklyn DA's office from fifty-six to thirty-nine.

And Gold ended Koota's policy of letting assistant DAs maintain private law practices. As a result, the assistants now work full time for the public. And unlike the old days, some of the top assistants and bureau chiefs in Gold's office don't even belong to political clubs.

Koota's handling of several cases while he was Brooklyn DA still looks suspicious to law enforcement officials and to those concerned with a standard of equal justice.

One is the famous George Whitmore case.

Whitmore—nineteen, black, and barely literate—was indicted for rape by Koota's office and for the sensational Wylie-Hoffert homicide by Frank Hogan's office. As new evidence was discovered, Hogan decided to dismiss the homicide indictment against him. But Koota asked the Manhattan DA not to dismiss the homicide indictment until after he had tried Whitmore for rape—apparently so the murder indictment might be used to influence the jury in the rape case. Hogan, to his credit, dismissed the indictment before the rape trial began. Hogan also is reported to have told Koota that if he needed the psychological pressure of a Manhattan murder indictment to convince a Brooklyn jury to convict Whitmore for rape, then he had no business trying Whitmore in the first place.

And in mid-December, in a powerful program on Channel 13's "51st State," Whitmore and reporter Selwyn Raab accused Koota of "suppressing evidence" in the case while Koota was district attorney. Raab discovered in Puerto Rico an eyewitness to the alleged rape, an eyewitness the DA's office was aware of. That eyewitness was never called to testify at the trial. Raab also discovered a detective's notebook that contained written evidence supporting the defense's case; this fact, too, was never brought out during Whitmore's trial.

Today George Whitmore, now articulate and in his late twenties, is still in prison, still insisting he is innocent, still asserting he was railroaded by the police and the DA.*

Someone Koota did not send to prison was organized crime big shot Hugh (Apples) McIntosh.

In 1965, during the Gallo-Profaci gang war, a Gallo associate was murdered on a deserted Brooklyn street. But one seventeen-year-old girl happened to see the underworld assassination and took down the license plate. The girl later picked McIntosh out of a police line-up. Despite the ex-

---

* In April of 1973, Whitmore was finally set free when Brooklyn Supreme Court Justice Irwin Brownstein dismissed the original indictment against him. Brooklyn DA Gold supported the action. Koota made no comment.

Gold appeared personally before Brownstein and argued that the facts of the case "are so contradictory . . . that conscience dictates that the conviction be set aside."

Judge Brownstein then told Whitmore, "You are a free man. You may go."

istence of an eyewitness who was willing to testify at a trial, DA Koota dismissed a grand jury's homicide indictment against Mafioso McIntosh because he didn't think he could get a conviction.

At about the same time he was dismissing the McIntosh indictment, DA Koota was doing a favor for Anthony Anastasia, the nephew of the notorious Mafioso Albert Anastasia.

On August 30, 1966, while DA of Brooklyn, Koota submitted an affidavit in praise of the fine moral character of Anthony Anastasia, who was then in a court fight to win custody of his two sons from the parents of his deceased first wife. Koota's affidavit was filed with the Oneida County Supreme Court in Utica. Koota's sworn statement described Anastasia as "a man of great personal integrity and honor."

The subject of Koota's tribute had been convicted of illegal entry on July 28, 1952, and at that time was reportedly listed by the Justice Department as a member of the Carlo Gambino organized crime family.

There was one situation while Koota was DA of Brooklyn in which he was almost indicted himself.

In 1964 there was a major scandal involving a conspiracy to rig bids on city paint contracts for the Housing Authority. A contractor named Jack Graham of Wantagh, Long Island, wouldn't go along with the conspiracy and was savagely beaten with tire irons by hoods. When he got out of the hospital, Graham went to Aaron Koota and told him the whole story of the rigged bids.

Koota was then running for DA and was head of the Rackets Bureau. Several months passed, and Koota had not started an investigation. So Graham went to Joe Phillips, an assistant in Frank Hogan's office, with the same set of facts.

Hogan's office began an investigation that quickly led to the indictment of Martin Rarback, the president of the Painters' Union, and several contractors for the City Housing Authority.

One of the indicted Housing Authority conspirators was Sam Esrig. Esrig told Hogan's investigators he had given some money to his co-conspirators for a payoff to the Brooklyn DA's office to kill any investigation of the conspiracy.

During the trial of Rarback, Esrig, and the others, prosecutor Phillips tried to introduce testimony into evidence about the subconspiracy to bribe the Brooklyn DA's office. On February 16, 1968, in open court, there was a bitter debate between Phillips and Judge Irwin Davidson on whether to permit testimony on this point. Judge Davidson refused to let the jury hear it, and the information never became public.

According to a person close to the investigation, after the trial was over one of the other guilty defendants admitted that a bribe was paid to kill any investigation in Brooklyn.

Koota's concern for the civil liberties of dope dealers and mobsters does not seem to extend to ordinary citizens. While he was Brooklyn DA, Koota gave several widely reported speeches attacking the decisions of the Earl Warren Supreme Court. In August, 1967, DA Koota said he would "continue to wiretap," even though the Supreme Court had ruled New York's bugging laws unconstitutional.

Koota's insistence on illegal electronic eavesdropping motivated Charles Desmond, the former chief judge of the Court of Appeals, to make a speech criticizing Koota for "lawless law enforcement."

"Tell our prosecutors they are our servants and not our masters," Judge Desmond told a session of the Constitutional Convention.

Koota also made frequent speeches attacking the Supreme Court's decisions on the rights of suspects and on limits on the use of confession. In a television interview in September, 1966, Koota said: "These recent Supreme Court decisions have shackled law enforcement agencies, making it possible for vicious criminals to escape punishment. . . . The Warren Court favors the fox-hunt theory of law enforcement, in which the fox is given a sporting chance to escape."

And in the October 9 edition of *The New York Times*, Judge Koota gave a rather clear picture of his judicial mentality. The week before, the *Times* had published several stories detailing how blacks, Puerto Ricans, and defendants too poor to hire their own attorneys consistently received longer prison sentences than more affluent whites, including members of organized crime. This disparity of sentencing included statistics from the Federal Bureau of Prisons that showed the average prison sentence for whites was 42.9 months, for blacks and Puerto Ricans, 57.5 months. The *Times* also reported that defendants who could not afford their own counsel were sentenced nearly twice as severely as defendants with private lawyers.

When asked to comment on this apparent bias based on class and race, Judge Koota told the *Times* reporter: "Our Constitution has never guaranteed equality among all people. It only guarantees equality of opportunity. My experience has indicated there is no disparity based on affluence. True, more severe sentences are placed on minority groups. But that's because of the type of crimes they commit. You never heard of a bank president going out and mugging somebody."

I have ended several of these articles with appeals to those in authority—Presiding Justices Rabin and Stevens, Chief Judge Fuld—asking them to begin their own inquiries into the facts of these cases. It now seems clear that I was naive. These three prestigious jurists appear to have no motivation, no zeal, to clean their own house. All three are good judges, but they are terrible administrators.

The evidence of judicial misconduct is abundant. Special State Prosecutor Maurice Nadjari has already said there are "more than twenty judges" under active investigation by his office. Judge Joseph Corso has recently been questioned by a Brooklyn grand jury and is under scrutiny by DA Gold's office. The Joint Legislative Committee on Crime has released statistics documenting a pattern of leniency by judges toward members of the Mafia and toward heroin dealers, especially in Brooklyn.

In the face of all this smoke, Presiding Justice Rabin of Brooklyn has displayed no interest in searching for any fire.

The late State Senator John Hughes often made the point that it was unwise to expect judges to judge other judges. And the record supports his opinion.

On January 17, 1971, the *Times* published a story announcing that the Appellate Division, Second Department, was looking into an allegation of misconduct against Queens

Civil Court Judge Kenneth Brown. But nothing ever happened. A few months later, a journalist called Justice Rabin's office to check on the progress of the inquiry and was told there never was one.

Every law enforcement agency in the state is aware of Judge Dominic Rinaldi's reputation for going easy on members of the Mafia. The Joint Legislative Committee on Crime has a whole file full of suspicious dispositions by Rinaldi in organized crime cases. But apparently Justice Rabin has not had the curiosity to look any deeper into the matter.

And then there is the case of Brooklyn Civil Court Judge Ross Di Lorenzo. Di Lorenzo took the Fifth Amendment before a federal grand jury when asked whether he had tried to fix an organized crime case. Judge Di Lorenzo appears, from the transcript, to have lied four times during a hearing before an Appellate Division referee when asked about the same case.* Judge Di Lorenzo also violated the Canons of Judicial Ethics by participating in a fund-raising event for Mario Procaccino during the 1969 campaign.

Despite all this, Presiding Justice Rabin merely reprimanded Di Lorenzo and let him remain on the bench.

Justice Rabin, the most powerful jurist in all of Brooklyn, Queens, Nassau, and Richmond, is treated like a king in the courthouse. Everyone in the judicial system, from typist to judge, speaks of him and to him with great deference.

But Rabin is just another politician with a black robe. He is a former Republican assemblyman. He was not appointed presiding justice by an independent screening panel or by

---

* On August 9, 1973, Judge Di Lorenzo was indicted for perjury. The indictment was based on this same transcript.

vote of his peers. He was appointed by Nelson Rockefeller as part of the normal commerce of political favors because he happens to be a Republican.

For weeks I tried to arrange an interview with Justice Rabin; he wouldn't even come to the phone. Last December, my colleague Mary Perot Nichols asked for an interview with Justice Rabin on the Di Lorenzo case. She was told by his clerk that the request for an interview was denied.

And while ducking the press and doing nothing to investigate any of the suggestions of judicial misconduct, Justice Rabin and the other presiding justices have hired a public relations firm (Ruder & Finn) to advise them how to get more favorable publicity from the major media.

In these articles on the judiciary I have tried to offer concrete examples of misconduct by judges—inadequate judgment, inadequate temperament.

There may or may not be actual corruption involved. I do not pretend to know. It is up to the various prosecutors —who have professional staffs, undercover agents, and the power to offer immunity—to assemble the evidence to prove the commission of a crime under the rules of evidence in a court of law.

What I am seeking to do is establish a standard for disciplining and removing judges based not solely on blatant corruption but on a reasonable measure of competence, integrity, and character.

It seems to me very difficult to prove a judge took money in a given circumstance. But if a judge has shown a clear pattern of leniency toward Mafia members and heroin dealers, and these permissive decisions were based on dubious law and were consistently overruled by higher courts, that seems to me plausible grounds for removal.

But in addition, one Supreme Court justice in Brooklyn has been drunk on the bench three of the last four times I visited his courtroom. Two Civil Court judges—one in Brooklyn and one in Queens—are emotionally unstable: shouting irrationally, throwing trantrums, abusing lawyers almost every day. Several other Brooklyn judges have an unmistakable prejudice against blacks and Puerto Ricans and do not give minorities equal protection of the laws.

None of these men—and they are all white males—has the right to sit in judgment of others. They are unqualified to be judges. But they are judges. And they feel sure no one will call them to account for their behavior.

My essential argument here is that the chain of accountability has broken down. And Presiding Justice Rabin is to blame.

Judges feel they are literally beyond the law. Lawyers are prohibited from criticizing them. Their colleagues are reluctant to be quoted against them. The DAs fear retaliation in the courtroom if they go public with their suspicions about certain judges. Most politicians aspire to become judges and so do not attack the system too vigorously. And the press does not systematically cover the courts, except when there is a sensational trial, and then they all converge on one courtroom.

The only way to hold judges accountable is tough and vigilant administration. Under the law, that is the responsibility of the presiding justices and the chief judge of the Court of Appeals.

In the cases of Judges Rinaldi, Di Lorenzo, Corso, and now Koota, Presiding Justice Rabin has behaved like an ostrich at an orgy, his head buried in the sand while the strangest things go on all around him.

December 28, 1972

POSTSCRIPT

On July 13, 1973, Gerald Martin Zalmanowitz testified before Senator Henry Jackson's Permanent Subcommittee on Investigations. Zalmanowitz, a government witness against organized crime and a convicted bond swindler, described the system of fixing cases while Aaron Koota was district attorney of Brooklyn (between 1964 and 1968).

Zalmanowitz told the Senate committee that he knew of "many fixed cases" but described only two—both involving organized crime.

"I was personally involved in one," Zalmanowitz testified, "where $5,000 was given to an attorney from the district attorney's staff. . . . This $5,000 was distributed among the various people in the district attorney's office. The case involved bootlegging cigarettes, and when the trial came, the defendant just walked out of the courtroom, even though he had a record of three prior convictions for the same thing."

Zalmanowitz said the second case involved Mafia boss Joe Colombo. He testified that Colombo wanted a delay in testifying at a certain trial, and this favor was purchased with a free Buick for Walter Buchbinder, then Koota's chief investigator. The Buick came from a Brooklyn dealership that Colombo indirectly owned.

In 1973, Buchbinder was indicted for receiving stolen property.

Zalmanowitz also told the Senate committee that the contact man for fixing cases in Koota's office was William Light. Light, who has a record of ten arrests and three convictions, was a campaign fund-raiser for Koota. His son, Martin Light, also worked in Koota's office, and he too is now under indictment.

When asked by *New York Times* reporter Ralph Blumenthal to comment on Zalmanowitz's testimony, Koota—now a Supreme Court justice—said, "I know the stories don't put me in a favorable light, but I'm completely satisfied with my own integrity of course. That's beyond question."

"Mindlessly, randomly, hurriedly, blindly"

IN RECENT WEEKS, testimony from five respected and unexpected witnesses has been offered in support of the cause of court reform. The sources of this testimony are a conservative state commission appointed by Governor Rockefeller and the party leaders of the state legislature; the final report of the Knapp Commission; a prominent federal judge; the man who prosecuted Lenny Bruce with such zeal; and the deputy chief inspector of the New York City Police Department.

The Temporary Commission on the State Court System was created by an act of the legislature in May, 1970. Its members included Clinton Dominick (chairman), the former Republican state senator from Newburgh; Charles Siegfried, president of the Metropolitan Life Insurance Company; Republican Assemblyman Edward Crawford of Oswego; Charles Desmond, the former chief judge of the state; Mrs. Charles Hubbard of the League of Women Voters; and Nathan Sobel, the current surrogate of Brooklyn and a most loyal member of the regular Brooklyn organization.

A commission with this membership might have been expected to draft a document that praised the existing court system or made suggestions of a repressive nature. But the commission's 200,000-word report, released in January, said it found "too much that is wrong" and went on to make sensible, humane recommendations for change: abolition of the cash bail system; abolition of judicial conventions to nominate Supreme Court justices (these are always controlled by the local political leaders); the creation of an independent commission—based on the California model— to investigate complaints against judges; and a new, permanent Court on the Judiciary, with the power to remove incompetent judges from the bench.

The surprisingly tough section on disciplining judges calls for "a permanent commission on judicial misconduct" to be composed of three judges appointed by the appellate departments, three lawyers appointed by the State Bar Association, and three laymen appointed by the governor. This commission would be empowered to investigate and censure judges.

Judges could be retired or removed by a permanent Court on the Judiciary for "misconduct in office." The report goes on specifically to define "misconduct" to include:

—laziness, such as starting court late, ending early, taking afternoons or days off;

—lack of patience with persons in court;

—rudeness and arbitrariness, such as shouting at, berating, or making derogatory comments about persons in court;

—improper use of alcohol;

—showing bias against certain races or classes of litigants;

—allowing personal considerations to influence judicial decisions;

—associations with persons [off the bench] that give rise to suspicions about partiality—for example, litigants, politicians, or reputed underworld figures;

—corruption in office.

It is these rigorous standards plus the new concept of making the Court on the Judiciary a permanent institution that are significant. Currently, no standing mechanism exists for holding judges accountable. A Court on the Judiciary can be convened, but it is a slow, cumbersome process involving considerable politics and clubbiness. Between 1947 and 1971, the court was convened only three times.

The Commission on the Court System goes on to observe: "There is a definite lack of communication between the appellate divisions in New York City, and those who feel judges have acted improperly. Given the conflicts built into the system, it is doubtful that the widespread lack of confidence in it can be eliminated without a major restructuring of the discipline system."

In polite language, this seems to be a deserved criticism of Presiding Justices Rabin and Stevens for their passivity and aloofness.

The 264-page final report of the Knapp Commission on police corruption is one of the most valuable and disturbing official documents I have ever read. Although it fails to locate ultimate responsibility for the "widespread and extensive corruption" it found, the report does provide staggering details, especially in the area of narcotics.

The Knapp Commission had no jurisdiction over the courts, and the staff made no effort to investigate judicial corruption; nonetheless, the report does comment on the courts in a little-noticed chapter (pages 249–56).

The Knapp staff went through the dispositions of ninety-one policemen convicted in criminal trials for corruption between 1968 and July, 1972. Of the eighty who had been sentenced, "49 were either set free or given suspended sentences, and 31 received jail terms, 14 for less than one year."

The report goes on to make this point:

It is clear that the risks of severe punishment for corrupt behavior are slight. A dishonest policeman knows that even if he is caught and convicted, he will probably receive a court reprimand, or at most, a fairly short jail sentence. Considering the vast sums of money to be made in some plainclothes squads, or in narcotics enforcement, the gains from corruption seem to far outweigh the risks.

As in most examples of suspicious judicial conduct, the Brooklyn judges were the worst. According to the Knapp report, nineteen police officers were convicted on corruption charges in Brooklyn between 1968 and 1972. Only three of the nineteen received more than one year in jail.

On February 3, Federal Judge Jack Weinstein spoke to the Columbia Law School alumni luncheon at the Commodore Hotel. His audience included about thirty judges, Frank Hogan, Whitney Seymour, Sr., and leaders of the

Bar. His subject was the discipline and removal of judges. Weinstein, who is also a Columbia law professor and one of the most brilliant jurists in the state, began: "New York's courts are in trouble. . . . For the last five years, while I have been on the federal bench, I have remained quiet while the situation in New York grew ever more desperate. . . . I can no longer in good conscience remain silent."

Weinstein then proposed the immediate formation of a statewide commission to investigate all charges of misconduct against judges; he proposed that "a majority of the commission should be laymen and lawyers, rather than judges. . . . The courts are too important to be left to judges and lawyers alone. The presence of laymen will increase public confidence in the discipline system, bring a fresh and different viewpoint to the discussions, and curb the natural reluctance of judges to condemn the conduct of their judicial brethren." This commission would have the power to censure judges.

Judge Weinstein also urged that the Court on the Judiciary be made permanent and that it have the power to remove and retire judges. He added, to the obvious discomfort of his audience, that the Appellate Division has failed in its responsibility to investigate judicial misconduct and that the public has lost confidence in that mechanism. "The public feels, and justifiably so," he said, "that all but the most serious complaints will be whitewashed or disposed of with a slap on the wrist."

Judge Weinstein concluded by departing from his text to say: "Those of you in this audience who have spoken to me privately about abuses and failures in the courts have the responsibility now to speak out in public. Those of you who know about absues and remain silent are among those most responsible for the way things are."

Richard Kuh served nine years as the administrative assistant to Manhattan District Attorney Frank Hogan; Kuh was the courtroom prosecutor in the obscenity trial of Lenny Bruce in 1964. Nevertheless, in the January 8 edition of the *New Leader,* Kuh published a detailed, almost bitter attack on the New York City court system.

Kuh, who knows the inner workings of the judiciary from daily experience, wrote that "there is much that is rotten about the selection of judges. . . . The overwhelming majority of them are mediocre."

Kuh also commented on the laziness of many judges. He described "the banker's hours, the funeral director's pace, the madhouse's inefficiencies, the jet-setter's frequency of holidays. . . . Bestowed as a reward for loyal party service, a place on the bench is seen as the most honorable sort of quasi-retirement."

Kuh then quoted approvingly from Police Commissioner Patrick Murphy's memorable 1971 speech to the Bar Association: "The court system must accept a giant share of the blame for the continual rise in crime. . . . It has broken down. Neither the innocent nor the guilty receive justice, for they are handled alike, mindlessly, randomly, hurriedly, blindly."

In his conclusion, Kuh echoed the need for two basic court reforms: "The power to remove judges, now scant indeed, should be extended, and far more liberally exercised." And "the selection of judges should be separated from party politics."

Kuh, however, did not try to answer the more problematic question of whether the new method of selecting judges should be appointive or elective. My tentative view on this point is that independent screening panels recommending judicial candidates on merit alone would be the best method, provided the screening panel was not dominated by upper-class corporate lawyers. To guarantee street-wise representation, I would, for example, let the Fortune Society and the Legal Aid Society each pick one member of the screening panel. Mayor Lindsay has introduced legislation in Albany that would let the governor, the presiding justices, and the Bar Association control the screening panel. I'm afraid that would exclude a necessary working-class skepticism from the process.

I would also go a step further and require that the presiding justices and administrative judges be nominated by independent screening committees. Right now, the PJs are appointed by the governor for political and patronage reasons that have nothing to do with their talents as managers or administrators.

On January 15, *The New York Times* published a one-column headline on page fourteen. It read, "POLICE DRUG AIDE ASSAILS JUDICIARY." The "police drug aide" was Deputy Chief Inspector William Bonacum, who is in charge of the department's Narcotics Division and has an impeccable reputation for honesty. Reporter John Darnton interviewed Chief Bonacum a few days after Governor Rockefeller had proposed mandatory life sentences, without possibility of parole, for all convicted drug sellers, including those arrested for selling hashish and LSD. Bonacum called Rockefeller's plan "completely unworkable."

Chief Bonacum's central point in the interview was that his cops were risking their lives, working for months undercover to make quality arrests, spending thousands of dollars in "buy" money, only to find the courts returning the major heroin dealers to the streets.

Bonacum produced official statistics that showed that in 1971, of the 20,762 persons arrested on felony narcotics charges, only 2 percent (418) were sentenced to more than one year in prison. In 1970, there had been more than 26,000 felony narcotics arrests, of which only 346—1 percent—had been sentenced to more than one year.

During 1972, cops working under Chief Bonacum made 4,000 felony narcotics arrests, with a determined emphasis on big heroin dealers. According to Bonacum, it cost the city's taxpayers about $10 million to make those arrests, including $900,000 just in "buy" money for undercover cops. He estimates that only 200 of the 4,000 will spend more than a year in prison. Of those narcotics dealers convicted in the special narcotics courts started last year, 67 percent did not serve any time in jail.

Chief Bonacum was angry enough with the leniency of judges to examine personally the court records of twenty-five random cases in which the defendant had been convicted of a narcotics felony and had not gone to jail. Of this sample twenty-five who went free, Bonacum found fourteen with prior arrests and of these, two with "a heavy arrest record."

Chief Bonacum has compiled a brochure on "the 100 top narcotics violators in the city." Almost all had been arrested within the previous twenty-four months. Last year, forty of the hundred were arrested by police and were nonetheless "back on the streets again," Bonacum said.

What all this fresh establishment testimony suggests is that the problem with the courts is deeper and more pervasive than merely the occasional extremities of scandal; the problem is also the general lack of fairness, reason, and dignity for the mass of defendants. The problem is not only that ten or fifteen judges fix cases, but that the whole system doesn't work. The city's courts are a broken meat-grinder. The sick junkie and the propertyless first offender get punished too harshly, while the big heroin dealer, the Mafioso, and the corrupt cop get treated too leniently. Justice is stood on its head.

On top of that, the system is saturated with clubhouse politics and is bereft of accountability.

The consequences of this twice-rotten system are neither remote nor abstract. The consequence of corruption is that heroin is slowly destroying a generation in the ghettos, and the fear of street crime by addicts is making New York a ghost town after the sun sets.

The dull, methodical failure of the courts can be seen most clearly every morning in Family Court, in Landlord-Tenant Parts, in the lower criminal courts. This is where the average defendant confronts the average judge. Just sit there any morning and you will see judges who regularly remand sixteen-year-old addicts to jail instead of paroling them to narcotics treatment programs like Phoenix House.

You will see judges who don't listen, judges who insult lawyers and defendants, judges who are not intelligent enough to follow complex or subtle legal argument, judges who are blatantly biased against blacks and Puerto Ricans, judges who call defendants names like "scum" and "animal."

You will see inexperienced Legal Aid lawyers represent fifty poor defendants in a day and not have time to ask more than their names beforehand. You will see defendants who have been in jail for nine months without seeing a judge, defendants who could have been paroled months earlier. You will see pleas and sentences delayed because probation reports are lost in a maze of bureaucracy. You will see heroin dealers in red jumpsuits post $25,000 bail in cash and addicts from Bed-Stuy locked up for a year because they don't have $50. And a cop convicted of selling heroin given a suspended sentence.

I have seen judges fine landlords $15 for 200 violations of the housing code, including failure to provide heat and hot water, and then have lunch with the landlord's lawyer. I have seen one judge sentence a Puerto Rican junkie to three years in prison for shoplifting some clothes, and another judge give probation to a white defendant who wore a suit and had a private lawyer and had been convicted of embezzling $150,000 from a bank.

It is only such obvious, systemic inequities that could persuade people like Judge Desmond and Clinton Dominick to propose reforms like removing incompetent judges and abolishing the cash bail system.

It is no longer a few radical lawyers or a few militant inmates who say the courts have little to do with justice. Those who know the criminal justice system best are saying it—

conservatives, who respect the law and despise corruption.

The late Republican State Senator John Hughes was the most knowledgeable advocate of court reform in the state. It was his Joint Legislative Committee on Crime that compiled all the original research documenting that members of organized crime and heroin dealers received more lenient sentences and won more dismissals than all other types of defendants. One study prepared by the Hughes Committee showed that of all those convicted (not just arrested) for possession of more than one pound of heroin or cocaine between January, 1969, and October, 1971, 40 percent received no jail sentence at all and 26 percent received less than one year in jail.

The final report of the Knapp Commission quoted this study and remarked, "The disposition of these cases appears disproportionately lenient in view of the fact that possession of one pound or more of these drugs became punishable by life imprisonment on April 24, 1970." Such permissive sentences are frustrating and demoralizing for the individual cop, the report went on to say, and contribute to the climate and attitude that permits corruption to flourish.

And it was the police commissioner of New York City who said of our court system, "Neither the innocent nor the guilty receive justice, for they are handled alike, mindlessly, randomly, hurriedly, blindly."

February 8, 1973

A Decent Judge in
a Rotten System

IT WAS 7:00 P.M., two nights before Christmas, 1972, in the Brooklyn House of Detention on Atlantic Avenue. In the basement of the jail, in a small room with peeling walls, a judge sat without a robe. The judge was calling the defendants "Mr." and "Sir." He would walk from behind the beat-up desk that was being improvised as a bench, and he would touch addicts and feel the needle scars on their arms.

It was freezing outside. The prison was jammed to 165 percent of capacity. And forty-two-year-old Irwin Brownstein was probably the only State Supreme Court judge in the whole city working that late. And he was working in his shirtsleeves in the bowels of the jail.

Martin Mayer is the director of the Court Referral Project, a city program that helps place heroin addicts in treatment facilities instead of letting them languish in jail waiting for trials.

"Brownstein might be the best judge in the city," Mayer was saying. "Most judges would rather throw a kid into

Rikers Island than put him into a narcotics treatment program. A few good judges will talk to us if we happen to have someone in the courtroom. But Brownstein is the only judge who will walk off the bench and call us to come interview a defendant, to see if he is a reasonable risk for a program. He'll even call me in the middle of the night, if he is brooding about a guy he saw the day before. He'll say, 'I had a second thought about this guy, maybe you can find a therapeutic community for him. . . .'

"But what I really respect about Brownstein is that he's not just a softie. If he gives a guy a chance, and the guy splits from a program, then he'll always give him the maximum sentence the next time around. Brownstein will give you that one chance, but if you fail, then he's always very tough. That's the right balance of attitudes."

For months I have been writing about bad judges. So last November I started looking for a good judge to interview. I understood that being a judge could be a difficult job filled with doubts and hard decisions: A judge sees the worst side of human nature every day. I knew that if you were an honest, serious judge, the job could give you ulcers and bad dreams. I wondered what it was like to be a decent judge inside a rotten system.

I had heard about a couple of excellent judges, but when I finally went to see them myself, they struck me as flawed —short-tempered, already broken by their deadening environment. But Judge Brownstein appeared intact—honest, fair, free of racial prejudice. And totally involved with his defendants as human beings. Defendants he sentenced would later come to his home for dinner and sometimes stay for a week until Brownstein found them a job. He helped start and furnish a narcotics treatment center in Rockaway. He corresponded with dozens of men he had sent to state prisons. He gave money out of his own pocket to men he had just paroled.

All of this seemed quite extraordinary, since Brownstein, who had risen in politics through the regular Brooklyn organization, is a close friend of the borough's political boss Meade Esposito. This clubhouse background has provided Brownstein with valuable street-smarts unavailable at Harvard Law School. (Esposito, when asked, described Brownstein as "a great fuckin' judge.") But then, one of the greatest of all the Supreme Court justices—Benjamin Cardozo —had been a child of Tammany Hall during the era of its most venal excesses. The world is still complicated. Even in Brooklyn.

I was recently talking to a federal prosecutor about the dimensions of court corruption. "Things are so bad in Brooklyn," he said, "that in the crunch, I can count on three judges, and Carlo Gambino can count on four."

"Who are the three you trust?" I asked.

"Brownstein, Vince Damiani, and Tom Jones."

I repeated this conversation to a bureau chief in the Brooklyn District Attorney's office. The chief said: "Brownstein is so honest he's always the first judge we ask to sign a search warrant or a court order for a wiretap, especially in organized crime cases. We wake him up in the middle of the night once a week. He's signed more warrants for us than any other Brooklyn judge. We bother him so much because we know we can trust him, that he won't tip the people we're trying to lock up."

I watched Brownstein's performance on the bench over a period of several months. During the two weeks he spent conferencing more than 200 cases in the Brooklyn jail, he did something very impressive. He paroled a sixteen-year-old Puerto Rican kid to Inwood House, a therapeutic community for addicts. He was taking a chance on the kid. On the way to Inwood House, the kid ran away.

But the next day Brownstein trusted his instincts again, and paroled a second youthful offender to Inwood House. The second kid is doing fine there. The first one is back in jail, on a warrant signed by Brownstein.

On another day Brownstein had a jury trial. The defendant was charged with resisting arrest and assaulting a cop. As the cop began to testify, it became apparent that Brownstein did not believe his version of the arrest. So Brownstein began to question the cop closely. Within twenty minutes it was clear to the jury that the cop was committing perjury, and the defendant was eventually acquitted.

Another jail case Brownstein heard involved a sixteen-year-old charged with burglary. The defendant had been in jail for nine months on $100 bail. He was young and scared. It was his first arrest. He told Brownstein he had gone into the apartment only to find shelter from the cold and had fallen asleep. Brownstein believed him, and paroled the kid. The kid walked out onto Atlantic Avenue and began to cry and dance.

The same day another defendant came before Brownstein. He was twenty-two and had been in the Brooklyn jail for a year charged with robbery. He had not seen a judge for seven months. He told Brownstein he was in jail on the day the alleged robbery took place. Brownstein checked this out, found it was true, and after a short speech about how crazy the criminal justice system is, paroled the defendant.

Later, Brownstein reluctantly paroled another defendant to NAAC, the state's program for addict-criminals. "I'm taking a chance with you," he said. "I hope I'm right. But I'm going to be here for a long, long time. If you split from NAAC, you'll go away for a long time. Look at me. I want you to understand that if you don't take this chance to straighten yourself out, if you ever come before me again, I will give you the maximum sentence. That is my policy. I have never made an exception."

At the end of the week I asked Brownstein why he went into the jail to conference more than 200 cases.

"I think the informality is helpful," he answered. "The courtroom is too intimidating. A defendant has just spent nine months in some insane detention facility. He hasn't talked to a lawyer in nine months. Suddenly they give him a Legal Aid lawyer he has never met before. Then they put him into a strange room, with a judge sitting high above him on a throne. He has to call him 'Your Honor.' And the judge is talking to him in legal language he doesn't understand. That's not the way to arrive at truth.

"In the jail I don't wear a robe intentionally, so I'm not such an authority figure. The inmate is more relaxed. It's his turf. The atmosphere isn't so formal and unfamiliar. I can talk to the defendant conversationally. It's just easier to ask a guy 'Did you do it?' or 'What's your problem?' in the jail situation."

At 2600 Seagirt Avenue in the Rockaway section of Queens is a Phoenix House where ex-junkies are rehabilitated. Justice Brownstein helped furnish that facility on his own time. I had heard this story and asked Brownstein about it.

"Oh, I had a lot of fun with that one," he said. "I almost got arrested the day we were moving in the new kitchen. I had visited that particular Phoenix House on Seagirt Avenue. It was filled with things that had been scavenged from abandoned buildings. So I convinced the owner of the Childs Restaurant across from the courthouse to donate a whole kitchen to the Phoenix House.

"One Saturday I got four guys I had placed on probation myself to come down to Court Street and help move all this heavy equipment—a bake oven, steam table, refrigerator, and grill. I called up a friend of mine who loaned us a forty-foot truck, and we started loading everything into it. The guys on probation kept asking me 'How ya doin', judge, baby?' as we moved all this heavy stuff. As we were loading the truck some guy stopped and started to make some nasty racial comments. I nearly got into a fight with him. But in the end nothing happened, and we got the whole kitchen transported in one day."

One night early in February I went out to Brownstein's house in Brooklyn and we talked about what makes a good judge.

"I think Jews generally make good judges because of the

Talmud," he began. "The Talmud teaches us justice and respect for the law, and compassion. I think that is why so many great judges, like Brandeis, were Jewish."

I knew about his policy of always giving a defendant the maximum possible sentence if he violated parole. I wanted to know if he had any other basic rules he always followed.

"Yes, two," Brownstein said. "I try to actually touch every addict I sentence. It reminds me of his humanity. That he is flesh and blood too; it serves to make me remember that he has a mother, a child, a wife, just like I do.

"My other basic rule is that in homicide trials I make the lawyers and the jury actually see pictures of the victim. In a sense, murder is a victimless crime, because there cannot be someone sitting in the witness chair to testify what the defendant did to him. That's why I insist there be photographs of the victim, so that the dead person will be a presence in the courtroom."

Late that night I asked Brownstein just how bad he thought the courts had become.

"Very bad. There are judges who don't belong on the bench. They are an embarrassment. . . . The judiciary has become the soft underbelly of the political process. There is clearly some corruption. The system does not work. NAAC doesn't work. The jails are barbaric. Probation reports get lost. Inmates wait nine months to see a judge. My caseload is overwhelming. I can't see any end to it. Whenever I criticize the system I get cautioned by some of my superiors that I should keep quiet. The whole concept of bail kills me. Nine out of ten defendants I see are black. None of them can raise $100 bail. I have defendants on my calendar who are in jail only because there is nobody to type the presentencing reports. I'm just depressed and frustrated all the time now. So is Tom Jones. So is any humane judge."

On February 22, Justice Brownstein announced his candidacy for chief judge of the Court of Appeals. His statement called for many reforms, including the removal of "intemperate, incompetent, and corrupt" judges from the bench.

After the press conference he said with some resignation: "Either I'm going to get elected chief justice, or else I'll just quit and go back to being a lawyer. I can't take this system any more unless I can change it."

March 1, 1973

POSTSCRIPT

Brownstein lost his campaign for chief judge. One reason for his defeat was that the state and city bar associations challenged his qualifications. Their decisions, however, revealed more about the mentality of the legal establishment than about Brownstein. The bar—particularly the state bar —is dominated by upper-class Republicans, mostly corporation lawyers, who have little daily experience in the criminal courts. Brownstein, a working-class maverick judge out of the Brooklyn organization, is an anathema to people like Whitney North Seymour, Sr.

After a period of depression, Brownstein has decided to remain on the bench—a good thing for the citizens of Brooklyn.

Scavengers of
the System

MOST middle-class citizens of New York City go through life never meeting a city marshal. But in the ghettos and *barrios,* on Sutter Avenue and on Fox Street, the marshals are feared and hated.

Marshals execute evictions of tenants for landlords. They garnish salaries, even welfare checks. They collect judgments for banks, loan companies, and credit companies. They repossess merchandise for department stores. They pull out gas and electric meters for utilities. They are the system's scavengers.

The individual marshals, like most people who get patronage jobs in politics, vary in quality from adequate to venal. The abuse is not personal but structural—it is the concept, the nature of the work itself.

Marshals are technically part of the Civil Court; they are accountable to the appellate divisions of the State Supreme Court. They are appointed by the mayor for six-year terms but are under no day-to-day scrutiny by any judicial, legislative, or executive official.

City marshals are private entrepreneurs working with the

authority of government. They receive no salary but take 5 percent of all the judgments they collect. They are given a badge and a gun by the government—and then work for institutions like Household Finance, Chase Manhattan Bank, CRUMCO, Goldman and Di Lorenzo,* Korvette's, Brooklyn Union Gas, and Con Edison. In theory, they are impartially performing the mandate of the Civil Court. In practice, they are the power elite's private money collectors.

A legal services lawyer recently told me this story of how the marshals function.

The lawyer's client—a Puerto Rican dishwasher—owed a department store $200. The dishwasher offered to pay in installments of $10 a week. The marshal illegally demanded a $75 down payment before accepting the installment arrangement. The dishwasher had to borrow $75 from a loan company to satisfy the marshal. Two weeks later, the dishwasher's child fell out of a window. There was a big doctor's bill. So he borrowed another $300 from the loan company. The marshal, suspecting he wouldn't get paid, then went to the dishwasher's boss to garnish his small salary. The boss, not wanting any trouble or extra paper work, fired the dishwasher.

One of the most basic inequities of the marshal system is that marshals usually do not help individuals who have won a court judgment against a business.

Small Claims Court is known as the "people's court" because a citizen does not require a lawyer to assert a claim

---

* A major real estate firm, Goldman and Di Lorenzo is widely rumored to have Mafia connections. It operates through management companies with regal names like Wellington and Imperial.

there. Between July 1, 1969, and June 30, 1970, some 21,000 judgments under $500 were awarded to New Yorkers in Small Claims Court. Of that number, fewer than 6,000 have actually been collected. This is because the marshals, who work for a percentage of the take, tend not to help the ordinary person who has a $100 judgment against a TV repair shop, a landlord, or a parking lot. The marshal will neglect that assignment and perform the more lucrative collections for landlords, loan companies, and banks. This is the class bias built into the system.

The City Charter lists no special qualifications for being a marshal—only an age of twenty-one and a residence in the city. They do not have to pass any civil service test. Almost all the existing seventy-one marshals got their jobs either through political connections, usually old-line Democratic district leaders or their families, or through John Lindsay's borough political associations.

Last year the marshals served 450,000 eviction notices, garnishments, and attachments of the Civil Court, collecting more than $3 million in legal fees. *Thirteen of them grossed more than $100,000 each in 1972.*

On October 5, 1972, city marshal Irving Sable was arrested on a charge of grand larceny by extortion. The city's Department of Investigation conducted the inquiry that led to his arrest. Sable had been appointed a marshal by Mayor Lindsay on July 12, 1971, and he had been recommended by several important old-line Brooklyn politicians.

Marshal Sable's lawyers quickly began judge-shopping in Brooklyn in an effort to maneuver the case before a sympathetic jurist. The case drifted from part to part on motions for several months. It eventually came to rest before Brooklyn Supreme Court Justice Harold McLaughlin. McLaughlin heard arguments on a defense motion to inspect and dismiss. He was then assigned to another part and took the case with him, something highly unusual, even in Brooklyn. Finally Justice McLaughlin threw out the two felony extortion indictments against Sable, leaving only a misdemeanor.*

This decision raised some suspicions. Justice McLaughlin's son also happens to be a city marshal. And his son happens to be a marshal with an office at the same address as Sable's—66 Court Street in Brooklyn.

One more interesting fact: Sable's son (Daniel Sable) is the law secretary to Brooklyn Supreme Court Justice Guy Mangano. And Guy Mangano's father is James Mangano, chief clerk of the Brooklyn Supreme Court and a force in borough politics since 1934, when he became a district leader in Red Hook. As chief clerk, Mangano controls about 150 patronage jobs. He is a very tough and mysterious man who does not seek publicity to confirm his power.

Like most of the Supreme Court justices in the borough of Brooklyn, Justice McLaughlin is very political. One night last autumn, George Meisner visited Judge McLaughlin's house and asked him to sign a court order staying the integration of Junior High School 211 in Canarsie. Meisner is a Democratic party district leader and the personal lawyer of County Leader Meade Esposito. McLaughlin naturally signed the court order. It was so incompetently drafted that an appellate judge vacated it six hours later.

* In October, 1973, Brooklyn DA Gold reindicted Sable on the two extortion counts. The case is now pending.

Justice McLaughlin went on the bench more than twenty years ago under the sponsorship of James Powers, the former chairman of the Board of Elections. Now sixty-eight years old, Justice McLaughlin has somehow managed to acquire personal wealth while in the political life. He owns a considerable amount of real estate in upstate New York. His son is a city marshal. He has prospered—like so many regular politicians in Brooklyn.

A short digression is necessary here to place the Brooklyn Democracy, judges like Harold McLaughlin, and marshals like Irving Sable, into some perspective and context.

Meade Esposito is an earthy, amusing, and complicated man. It has become the fashion lately in some circles to romanticize pols like Esposito as some "new breed of boss," as *The New York Times Magazine* recently described him in a favorable cover story.

I disagree with this tendency. It is based on two cynical premises. One is the barroom notion that personality can be a substitute for ideas and values; that if a Matty Troy is fun to hang out with, then he is a valuable leader, even if he endorses Mario Biaggi for mayor, even if he gerrymanders the City Council district lines so that Puerto Ricans remain powerless, even if he makes deals that put judicial robes on ignorant politicians.

The other cynical premise is that politics is just a game, in which no one gets hurt. But it is not. There are always real consequences on the fragile lives of ordinary citizens— people who are not affluent and who are not famous and who don't have the leisure to be witty over a $10 steak at Jimmy's Restaurant.

The greening of pols like Esposito and Troy is essentially elitist because it ignores how government affects people and neighborhoods. The issue—as with the marshal system—is institutional, not personal. Meade Esposito is an interesting person, but the Democratic party of Brooklyn is an instrument of vested economic interest—notably real estate and banking. It is not an instrument of tenants or poor people.

Every regular Brooklyn councilman except Howard Golden voted to kill rent control. Comptroller Abe Beame's votes on the Board of Estimate usually reflect what the real estate developers want. Beame's chief fund raiser in the 1973 mayoral primary is Abe (Bunny) Lindenbaum, the most influential—and most investigated—real estate lawyer in the city.

For years, Brooklyn State Senator Jeremiah Bloom was both a bank trustee and a member of the Senate Banking Committee. Brooklyn politicians in the legislature have always voted the way the lobbyists for the savings and loan associations asked them to. Esposito is now a "consultant" on retainer to the Kings Lafayette Bank. The ILA (International Longshoremen's Association) has moved its considerable pension fund to that bank. The Brooklyn Democratic organization banks its money there. And John Lynch, the Kings Lafayette's honorary board chairman, has long been chairman of the Brooklyn County Committee.

Kings Lafayette has been rewarded for its political connections with $8 million in interest-free, on-demand deposits from the state and city governments. Kings Lafayette is a relatively small bank, and $8 million of such discretionary funds is a disproportionately large share.

Most of this money comes from the state and can probably be traced to the odd-couple friendship between the Republican billionaire governor and the former bail bondsman, now Democratic county leader, Meade Esposito. For example, Kings Lafayette has $3.9 million from the state in pari-mutuel deposits. This is more than any other bank in the whole state has, including Chase Manhattan.

These interest-free accounts, while cheating the taxpaying public of interest, help the banks enormously in terms of reserve position, capacity to borrow from other banks, and freedom to make loans and investments.

The total surplus and capital funds at Kings Lafayette is only $16 million. So its actual viability is dependent on political influence, and the $8 million in state and city deposits.

On the day before all important elections, the Brooklyn machine takes money out of the bank and distributes it to district leaders for vote-buying on election day. John Lynch indiscreetly admitted to *New York Times* reporter Will Lissner that he personally supervised the disbursement of $40,000 in new $5 and $10 bills on election eve in 1969.

According to Lissner's story in the *Times* last year, Lynch said, "The money was transported under police guard in a black leather satchel, and each of the twenty-three district leaders, before receiving $1,500–$2,000, signed a receipt."

The New York Times also reported, on February 14, 1972, that the Kings Lafayette Bank has been giving loans to members of organized crime in spite of their bad credit risk and lengthy criminal records. More than fifty alleged Mafiosi have received loans from the bank during the previous ten years.

One of the loans was made to Carmine Persico, now serving a fourteen-year prison sentence. The Persico loan went into default. So did another Kings Lafayette loan to Gaetano Massotta, an alleged captain in the Carlo Gambino family. According to bank records, Alphone D'Ambrisio, listed as a member of the Colombo family, took out three loans totaling $15,000 and gave a different address for each loan. In 1963, a company owned by Carmine Lobardozzi, an alleged captain in the Gambino family, received a loan that went into default.

Most of the Mafia loans were rushed through with no effort made to verify information given about addresses or occupations or financial status. A majority were never paid back. Mob loansharks then made immense profits by putting the bank money on the street at interest rates of up to 200 percent.

Legislators elected by the Brooklyn organization are not independent human beings; on important matters they vote how they are told.

A typical example of this occurred in April, 1972, in Albany. A marketing control bill sought by the Teamsters Union and the beer wholesalers was defeated in the assembly by a vote of 72–45. A few lobbyists met the next day with the leaders of the legislature, including Stanley Steingut. One week later, the same bill was reconsidered and approved by a vote of 98–28.

After the vote, Brooklyn Assemblyman Harvey Streizlin told a *New York Times* reporter, "I'm still against it, but I voted for it. I was told to change my vote."

A few ambitious and shrewd men like Esposito and

Steingut rise in that system and become rich and powerful. They get Picassos as gifts from the governor, and they own successful insurance companies. Their friends become judges and court clerks and marshals; some get bank charters and bank directorships, others receive city contracts and Surrogate's Court patronage and lowered real estate assessments.

But the mass of people who live in Brooklyn do not profit from this system—they often get screwed by it. If they go into the courts with the wrong lawyer, they do not find justice. If they are poor and black and live in Fort Greene, their congressman is the bigoted and senile John Rooney. If they are Puerto Rican, they do not see even one of their countrymen holding any elected office in the whole borough.

Meade Esposito likes to use populist rhetoric. But when there was a vacancy this year on the City Council, he did not give that seat to a young local from the neighborhood. He gave that seat to a fifty-year-old millionaire named Fred Richmond who does not even live in Brooklyn. Fred Richmond "represents" the working people of Williamsburg and Greenpoint in the Council. But Fred Richmond actually lives at 25 Sutton Place in Manhattan.

Public office in Brooklyn is often not public but private; certain positions seem to be kept within the family, away from ordinary people without proper blood lines.

Last year State Senator Edward Lentol became a Supreme Court justice, despite the opposition of *The New York Times* and the City Bar Association. At the same time, his son Joseph became the new assemblyman from Williamsburg.

Stanley Steingut's son Bob is now the regular organization's candidate for councilman-at-large in Brooklyn.* Stanley Steingut's father Irwin was the Speaker of the Assembly.

James Mangano made his son a Supreme Court judge in 1968. Two other Mangano relatives hold patronage positions in the Brooklyn Supreme Court.

Frank Cunningham is the most important district leader in John Rooney's congressional district. He is also the chief clerk of the Supreme Court's Appellate Term. His father was the district leader and alderman before him. His son is now a court clerk in Brooklyn.

And Justice McLaughlin's son is a city marshal. And Irving Sable's son is the law secretary to Justice Mangano.

The system in Brooklyn creates its own morality. Elections can be stolen. Judges can be fixed. Assemblymen can be told how to vote. Council seats can be bought. And city marshals are political cronies who do dirty work. If they get into trouble, the system's morality says you get them off because they are part of the club.

The problem is that in Brooklyn, about 15,000 people are in the club. And about two million citizens are outside it.

Marshals have always been tempted by greed and power.

During the 1930s, Mayor La Guardia tried to clean up the marshal system. He fired sixteen marshals for graft, and, under threat of indictment, eighteen more returned their guns and badges.

In 1935, La Guardia's commissioner of accounts, Wil-

---

* In the June primary, Bob Steingut secured the nomination, which effectively guaranteed him the position. He was elected in November, 1973.

liam Herlands, released a devastating report on the marshals. It said in part:

> Our inquiry has indicated that the marshals are for the most part uneducated and unfamiliar with the law governing their office. . . . Almost all are appointees of district leaders and have no special qualifications, except party affiliations.
>
> For years, a system of corrupt practices has grown up which has become so extensive that if a lawyer wants a marshal to act quickly in any given situation, he has to pay an excess fee for such action, although these excess fees are specifically prohibited by statute.
>
> The marshals have become so accustomed to receiving extra sums for their work that they often refuse to act in the cases of poor clients.

Last year the city's Department of Investigation received more than 400 formal complaints against marshals. This is more than it received against housing inspectors, meat inspectors, or any other type of city employee.

These citizen complaints covered a wide variety of abuses. There were allegations of property being stolen during evictions—from people with the most meager belongings. There were charges of court warrants for evictions being forged. There were claims of kickbacks to cops, to lawyers, to process servers. There were reports of illegal evictions performed with no court authority. There were dozens of complaints that marshals demanded money under the table to collect judgments for individuals. And there were dozens of complaints that marshals took a fee—and then did no work.

The Knapp Commission report made reference to a pattern of marshals paying money to cops to help with tenant evictions.

And a city marshal from Brooklyn—Joseph Spadaro of 105 Court Street—was recently named a co-conspirator by the Special Grand Jury that indicted Norman Levy for forgery and conspiracy in the fixing of parking tickets.

The mayor, however, has no power to suspend Spadaro, even though he appointed him. A marshal can be suspended or removed only by the Appellate Division. In the case of marshal Sable, who had been indicted for a felony, it required weeks of intense pressure from the city to force the Appellate Division to ask for Sable's gun back.

Four years ago the Citizens Union published a pamphlet attacking the marshal system. It was called "A Puddle of Political Patronage." Being appointed a marshal is indeed the prize patronage plum of them all. There are no tests or requirements. There is a great deal of money to be made. There are a gun and badge to guarantee respect.

Almost all the current seventy-one marshals are active in clubhouse politics. Their appointments were a reward for blind loyalty; objective qualifications have nothing to do with the honor.

One marshal owned a private detective agency when he was appointed. Another ran his own loan company. Others had such occupations as bartender, auctioneer, and process server. Although familiarity with the law is crucial to the job, fewer than 15 percent are lawyers.

Philip Sica, one of the thirteen marshals who grossed more than $100,000 last year, won his badge by running a storefront for John Lindsay in Queens during the 1965 campaign. Herbert Klein and Abe Friedman, two others who grossed over $100,000, are both active in regular Brooklyn politics.

The mayor's office has a little-known committee that is supposed to screen and approve all marshal appointments. The part-time executive director of that committee is David Arens. (Arens also has a private law practice.)

Last November David Arens was the Republican-Conservative candidate for Civil Court in Manhattan's Ninth Judicial District. He was expected to win. But ten days before the election, the Bar Association gave Arens the most bluntly negative rating of any judicial candidate in recent memory. The Association said of the mayor's good-government watchdog, "Not approved for lack of candor by reason of failure to disclose relevant information of detrimental nature bearing upon his qualifications to serve as a member of the Judiciary."

According to a member of that Bar Association committee, Arens had been questioned by a grand jury about his role in the 1967 James Marcus bribery scandal. Arens did not choose to disclose this bit of information to the committee that interviewed him.*

Mayor Lindsay's attitude toward the marshal system has been typical: noble intentions, heroic rhetoric, and ambivalent performance.

In 1968 Lindsay came before the Bar Association to give

* A week after this article appeared, Arens was asked to resign, and Lindsay issued a press release attacking the marshal system but did nothing to change it.

one of the best speeches of his career, a speech that ended with a summons to the legal profession to abolish the marshal system. "Almost every form of avarice and bullying can be found at some place in the history of the marshals," Lindsay said. He then quoted Edmund Burke: "People crushed by law have no hopes but from power. If laws are their enemies, they will be enemies to laws; and those who have much to hope, and nothing to lose, will always be dangerous."

And for the next four years, Lindsay honorably refused to appoint a single new marshal. But in April of 1971, Lindsay suddenly abandoned his opposition to the marshals, and since then he has appointed, or reappointed, fifty-one of them.

The pattern is uncomfortably reminiscent of the City Tax Commission—another quasi-judicial body. Lindsay promised to abolish the Tax Commission during one of his reform periods. Then he appointed Norman Levy—his chief political campaign fund raiser—to determine real estate assessments during a period of hard-nosed politics. (Levy has since been indicted.) Here he spoke eloquently for abolition. And after losing interest in that cause, he appointed a political operator to monitor a system saturated with politics to begin with.

Lindsay's good intentions, however, deserve some acknowledgment. In contrast, former Mayor Robert Wagner appointed twelve marshals on his last day in office in 1965. One was the son-in-law of the head of the Marshals Association, another was the son of a judge, and a third was a relative of a district leader.

There always has been—and probably always will be—
a certain level of corruption in government and politics.
It is where a lot of money can be made and where a lot of
dubious characters flourish.

Graft and greed are particularly endemic to the marshal
system because of the way it is conceived. The fee structure, the high incomes, the lack of any job requirements or
public scrutiny, the kind of private economic interests that
hire the marshals, the purely political method of selecting
—all reinforce the essential misconception of the job.

There is no way to reform such a system. It needs to be
completely dismantled and replaced with a whole other
mechanism.

Probably the soundest alternative would be to transfer
the marshal's role to the sheriff's office. The sheriff's depu-
ties are hired on merit from the Civil Service list and are
not clubhouse hacks. Their salaries are fixed by law. In
addition, the sheriff should become an appointed officer
directly accountable to the mayor.

Among those most responsible for the breakdown of the
marshal system are the appellate divisions of the State Supreme Court. These superior judges just looked the other
way, taking no interest in rooting out misconduct despite
those 400 citizen complaints last year.

The marshal system is the microcosm, the small, special
prism through which we can see with piercing clarity so
much of what is wrong with this city. The excessive power
of landlords, utilities, and banks. The enduring venality of
the clubhouse politicians. The lack of equal justice for poor
people in the courts.

Perhaps if the sheriff's office were made part of the

Bureau of Consumer Affairs and included some cops like David Durk, then it could become an instrument of truly equal justice.

Perhaps it could be used to collect court fines from slum landlords for violation of the housing code, to collect fines from air and water polluters and from businesses that cheat consumers.

I wonder what would happen if the people on Fox Street and Sutter Avenue suddenly saw the possibility of the law being applied equally—if they actually saw a sheriff's deputy arresting a landlord instead of evicting a tenant.

Law and justice and equality are majestic concepts. It is time they began to have some meaning in this city's communities of pain. One way to start giving them some credibility on the street is to abolish the marshal system.

March 29, 1973